King & Milk

Adam Black

King & Milk Snakes

Project Team
Editor: Thomas Mazorlig
Copy Editor: Stephanie Fornino
Cover Design: Mary Ann Kahn
Design: Mary Ann Kahn

T.F.H. Publications
President/CEO: Glen S. Axelrod
Executive Vice President: Mark E. Johnson
Publisher: Christopher T. Reggio
Production Manager: Kathy Bontz

T.F.H. Publications, Inc.
One TFH Plaza
Third and Union Avenues
Neptune City, NJ 07753

Copyright © 2007 by T.F.H. Publications, Inc.

All rights reserved. No part of this publication may be reproduced, stored, or transmitted in any form, or by any means electronic, mechanical or otherwise, without written permission from T.F.H. Publications, except where permitted by law. Requests for permission or further information should be directed to the above address.

Printed and bound in China,
07 08 09 10 11   1 3 5 7 9 8 6 4 2

Library of Congress Cataloging-in-Publication Data
Black, Adam, 1974-
King & milk snakes : a complete guide to Lampropeltis / Adam Black.
p. cm.
Includes bibliographical references and index.
ISBN 978-0-7938-2892-0
1. Lampropeltis as pets. I. Title. II. Title: King and milk snakes.
SF459.S5B58 2007
639.3'96—dc22
2007003980

This book has been published with the intent to provide accurate and authoritative information in regard to the subject matter within. While every reasonable precaution has been taken in preparation of this book, the author and publisher expressly disclaim responsibility for any errors, omissions, or adverse effects arising from the use or application of the information contained herein. The techniques and suggestions are used at the reader's discretion and are not to be considered a substitute for veterinary care. If you suspect a medical problem consult your veterinarian.

The Leader In Responsible Animal Care For Over 50 Years!™
www.tfh.com

Table of Contents

With the popularity that reptiles are experiencing as more mainstream pets, people are overcoming irrational fears or preconceived notions about these creatures as they become exposed to them. This is especially true with what has been traditionally the most feared and misunderstood of all reptiles: the snake.

To some, keeping a snake in one's home was once enough reason to consider someone insane. Today, more and more people accept snakes as beautiful creatures that play a beneficial role in the environment, and therefore more people want to enjoy snakes in their home. Some evidence for this is that the steadily growing number of professional and hobbyist reptile breeders is barely able to keep up with the rising annual demand for captive-produced snakes.

Kingsnakes and milk snakes (genus *Lampropeltis*) are among the most popular of pet snakes. Corn snakes and ball pythons are probably the only

Introduction

other species more popular and available in larger numbers annually than the California kingsnake. Many other species of kings and milks are also available in large numbers. A wide variety of kingsnakes and milk snakes is available in a vast array of natural colors and patterns. Breeders have selected superior individuals and even produced colors and patterns far removed and often more beautiful than those found in the wild. As snakes go, members of this group are relatively easy to keep in a simple setup. For those wishing to take snake ownership to the next level, many species of *Lampropeltis* are very easy to breed. Producing your own snake hatchlings can be a rewarding experience, and it also can be profitable.

If you have a king or milk snake or you are thinking of keeping one as a pet, you will find plenty of information in this book that will help you keep one healthy and content. You also will find information on the natural history of these beautiful snakes. Lastly, you will learn how to breed your snakes so that you can pursue that part of the hobby, if you decide to do so.

Chapter 1

Natural History

Most kingsnakes and milk snakes kept as pets were hatched in captivity. Despite this, they cannot be considered domestic animals. All pet snakes are still essentially wild animals, adapted to live in their native environment. Successfully keeping (and breeding) these snakes depends on knowing their natural history and duplicating necessary environmental conditions.

Herp Is the Word

Throughout this book, you will see the term "herp." This word refers to both reptiles and amphibians together. "Herp" comes from the word "herpetology," which is the study of reptiles and amphibians. When speaking about the hobby of keeping reptiles and amphibians, you can call it the "herp hobby." "Herpetoculture" is the keeping and breeding of reptiles and amphibians. A "herper" is someone who participates in the herp hobby or herpetoculture (also called a herp hobbyist).

Scientific and Common Names

Beginning with Carl Linnaeus in 1758 and continuing today, taxonomy, or literally "law of arrangement" is the science of organizing all living things by similar features. In modern times, biologists do this to identify evolutionary relationships.

As an example, a Pueblan milk snake would be classified as follows:

Kingdom: Animalia (animals)
Phylum: Chordata (possessing a spinal cord)
Subphylum: Vertebrata (possessing a backbone)
Class: Reptilia (Reptiles)
Order: Squamata (Snakes and Lizards)
Suborder: Serpentes (Snakes)
Family: Colubridae
Subfamily: Colubrinae
Genus: *Lampropeltis*
Species: *triangulum*
Subspecies: *campbelli*

Every organism described by a member of the scientific community is given a scientific name, which is normally in Latin. All kingsnakes and milk snakes belong to the genus *Lampropeltis*. Therefore, the only difference in the scientific names of kingsnakes will be within the last two categories, species and subspecies. When referring to a snake's scientific name, only the genus, species, and subspecies are used. Some species don't have any subspecies. The genus and species names should always be in italics when written. The first letter of the genus name is always capitalized, and the first letter of the species and subspecies is always in lowercase.

The genus *Lampropeltis* is a combination of "*lampros*," which means "shiny," and "*pelta*," which means "shield" (referring to scales). This appropriate name obviously refers to the smooth, glossy scales that all members of the genus have.

This taxonomical organization and the status of the scientific names used in this book are all subject to disagreement, depending on which research one agrees with. Continued studies of this genus and its relatives using modern methods will prove or disprove the current models of classification.

Common Names

Common names, which are employed outside of the scientific community, are not used scientifically due to a variety of localized names that creates confusion between speakers around the world. Additionally, some common names could refer to more than one animal. For example, does "green treefrog," refer specifically to *Hyla cinerea*, the small greenish treefrog of the eastern US, or does it refer to one of several other treefrog species that also have green coloration? When purchasing or looking for information on a particular king or milk snake, it is most helpful to know the current common and scientific names; knowing a recently outdated name is also useful.

The genus *Lampropeltis* is Greek for "shiny shield," referring to the snake's glossy scales. A Chihuahua mountain kingsnake is pictured.

The common name "kingsnake" is derived from the fact that snakes are a component of their natural diet. They are able to overpower and consume snakes of nearly identical size, including venomous species, thereby earning their title as "king."

Milk snakes earned their common name due to an absurd myth. It was thought that milk snakes came into barns to steal milk from cows. The presence of milk snakes around barns attracted to the presence of rodents probably accounts for the origin of this myth.

Distribution and Habitat

Kingsnakes are exclusively found in the Americas, ranging from southeastern Canada throughout much of the United States and down through Central America to the northern half of South America. The milk snake (*Lampropeltis triangulum* ssp.) is the widest ranging species and occupies this entire range.

With such a wide-ranging genus, the snakes utilize a variety of habitats. Various subspecies are adapted to their own habitat, which can range from arid deserts to wet rainforests. Some are lowland species, while others live only at high elevations. Some utilize land altered by humans, especially agricultural areas that tend to have an abundance of rodents. Kingsnakes often can be found under human garbage such as wood piles, old carpet, and pieces of tin. They generally are ground dwellers, but some species have been known to climb and bask in low branches.

Kingsnake Names

Milk snakes are all subspecies of one wide-ranging species (*Lampropeltis triangulum*), while all other *Lampropeltis* are referred to as kingsnakes. People often refer to snakes of the *Lampropeltis* genus collectively as "kingsnakes and milk snakes." Because both kings and milks are closely related and have similar captive requirements, this book will refer to them in most cases as just "kingsnakes" from this point forward to make things simple. Adding further confusion, herpers seem to prefer "kingsnake" as one word, although it is commonly written as two words (king snake). "Milk snake" is most often two words, although some spell it as one word (milksnake). According to Webster's Dictionary, both names are listed as two words. This is something to keep in mind if doing Internet searches for a particular snake, because you may get different results when searching both ways. This book will follow what seems to be generally accepted among the herp crowd, spelling "kingsnake" as one word and "milk snake" as two words.

Features of Kingsnakes and Milk Snakes

In comparison with other similar snakes in their native range, members of the genus *Lampropeltis* have smooth rather than keeled scales—scales with a raised ridge along the midline—with each dorsal scale bearing two sensory pits (apical pits). The anal plate (large scale just in front of the vent) is undivided, unlike in many similar snakes that have a divided anal plate. Other less evident anatomical features, such as skeletal characteristics, further differentiate members of the genus *Lampropeltis* from other snakes.

So what features separate a kingsnake from a milk snake? All milk snakes belong to the wide-ranging *Lampropeltis triangulum* complex of subspecies. In most cases, milk snakes have alternating bands or blotches of red, black, and yellow or white. Species with these markings are often referred to as "tricolors." However, these easily can be confused with various tricolor subspecies of mountain kingsnakes (*Lampropeltis zonata* ssp. and *Lampropeltis pyromelana* ssp.), and certain species of the *Lampropeltis mexicana* complex also have tricolor representatives bearing the common name "kingsnake." To make matters more confusing, one milk snake (*L. triangulum*) subspecies bears the common name scarlet kingsnake, even though all remaining *L. triangulum* are referred to as milk snakes. Some internal anatomical differences exist as well. Clearly, the division between kingsnakes and milk snakes is small, and this illustrates one more reason why scientific names are more accurate than common names.

Sensory Abilities

Despite common belief, most snakes have fairly good eyesight. When getting ready to shed, a snake's eyes become a cloudy blue-gray color, and this can temporarily compromise its eyesight. Many people believe that snakes cannot hear because they lack ears, but they do have the ability to sense low-frequency sounds and vibrations.

Perhaps the most remarkable sensory ability unique to certain reptiles is best described as equivalent to the combination of tasting and smelling in humans. Snakes don't have a tongue with taste buds, nor are they able to smell as mammals do. Instead, they use their forked tongue to pick up various chemical scents off surfaces around them. The tongue is then drawn into the mouth, and the scent molecules are analyzed by a specialized organ in the roof of the snake's mouth called the Jacobson's organ, also known as the vomeronasal organ. Snakes often can be seen flicking their tongue at their surroundings, especially when traveling in new locations. This important sensory ability can recognize certain scents, such as pheromones from potential mates and competitors of the same sex. The snake also uses this organ for finding food and perhaps for recognizing different localities in its home range.

Coloration

Many kingsnakes and nearly all milk snakes have alternating bands or blotches that extend from the neck to the tip of the tail. The most common theme is the tricolor appearance, in which there are alternating bands of black, red, and yellow, or black, red, and white. In some subspecies, the red coloration may appear more brown or orange than true red. Other kings from the

Although primarily ground dwellers, kings and milks, such as this New Mexico milk snake, will climb occasionally.

Lampropeltis mexicana complex may be highly variable, with dark patterns arranged in bands, blotches, or spots on a uniform lighter colored background color of gray to tan or orange.

Members of the *Lampropeltis getula* complex are widely variable. Some may be almost completely black, while others are speckled, blotched, banded, or striped. Usually they feature some combination of black patterning on a lighter background or light patterning on a predominantly black background.

Diet

Kingsnakes get their name from their habit of eating other snakes. This is referred to as being "ophiophagous," or snake eating. Remarkably, kingsnakes are able to swallow a snake nearly as long as they are, using muscular movements to fold the oversized meal in half within its stomach. Kingsnakes also are able to overpower and eat venomous snakes due to their immunity to their venom. Kingsnakes of the *Lampropeltis getula* complex seem to be the most ophiophagous of all the *Lampropeltis*. They will also eat nearly any terrestrial vertebrate they can catch, including small mammals, birds, lizards, frogs, and even baby turtles.

Many of the other species of *Lampropeltis* seem to prefer lizards or rodents as the primary part of their diet. Some feed almost exclusively on lizards in the wild, especially those species found in arid places. These snakes are often difficult to train to eat rodents in captivity. Neither kingsnakes nor milk snakes seem to bother eating invertebrates such as worms, insects, slugs, etc.

Periods of Activity

Most kingsnakes are active only when seeking food, looking for a mate, or

Kingsnakes are famous for eating venomous snakes. Here, an eastern kingsnake is feeding on a water moccasin.

regulating their body temperature. They spend the rest of the time hiding in a secure place away from predators. Because reptiles are cold-blooded (or more properly, ectothermic), they rely on their environment to warm or cool their bodies. Therefore, they must bask in the sun to warm up and retire in a hole to cool off.

Most kingsnakes are crepuscular, which means that they are active at dawn and dusk. In the early morning hours, they usually come out of hiding and bask in the first rays of sunlight to warm up after a cool night. After it is sufficiently warmed, the snake will retire to a cooler location, such as a hole, rotten log, pile of rocks, etc. If it wants to be cooler, it will seek out a spot deeper in the earth, but if it needs to be warmer, it will come closer to the surface. This ability to regulate body temperature is called behavioral thermoregulation. For most of the day during warmer months, the snakes will stay hidden during the heat of the day. Once the sun goes down, they will emerge again and remain active until it becomes too cool. Most snakes seem to travel the greatest distances in the evening hours.

During the winter, a snake will go into the reptilian equivalent of hibernation, called brumation. Triggered by cooler temperatures, a snake's metabolism will slow down considerably. It will not eat during this time and will wait out the winter buried underground or in piles of debris that are deep enough to prevent it from being exposed to freezing temperatures. These snakes will not go to sleep like hibernating mammals do but will still remain alert. However, body movements will slow down considerably. Brumation is usually required to stimulate breeding activity once the weather warms up the following spring.

Reproduction

Although some snakes bear live young, all kingsnakes are oviparous, which means that they lay eggs. Some species tend to lay more eggs per clutch than others, with clutches as small as a few eggs to more than 20 eggs per clutch, and a few exceptional individuals regularly lay more than 30 eggs per clutch. Most species average between 5 and 15 eggs per clutch. As a general rule, older and larger females lay more eggs than younger and smaller ones.

Breeding occurs shortly after snakes emerge from brumation, which coincides with springtime. Eggs are layed a few months after successful copulation in a slightly damp place, such as within a rotting log. The eggs incubate for about two months and then hatch. Neither parent stays with the eggs as some other types of snakes do. The hatchlings are entirely self-sufficient upon hatching.

Snakes may lay two or sometimes three clutches in one season. Those that tend to lay three clutches are usually from areas that have extended warm seasons.

Growth and Shedding

Growth rate is primarily dependant on food availability. A snake in the wild usually will grow much slower than a snake in captivity. This is due to the fact that most keepers feed their snakes readily, and because most captive snakes are kept warm (and therefore feeding) year round unless they are going to be brumated for breeding. Wild snakes rarely ever get as much food as snakes receive in captivity.

Shedding is a necessary part of growth. It also helps in healing injuries and ridding the body of external parasites. When shedding is imminent, fluids are secreted between the old outer layer of skin and the new layer underneath. This fluid often creates a blue-gray or cloudy appearance. A snake exhibiting this state is commonly referred to as being "opaque" or "in the blue." Shortly before shedding, this coloration will disappear and the snake will begin removing the old skin from its body. This shedding process also is known as ecdysis. The snake will start by rubbing its nose on any object around it to loosen the skin from around the upper and lower lip. From there, it will continue to work the skin off its body by rubbing against objects, peeling the skin off the body from head to tail. Usually the skin comes off in one piece and is inside out.

Longevity

The ages of wild snakes are impossible to determine. Therefore, average life spans only can be determined by captive specimens of known ages. Snakes kept in optimum captive conditions will most likely live significantly longer than wild specimens that are constantly

Kingsnake Complexes

You will note that some kingsnakes are listed as part of a particular "complex." In this regard, a complex refers to all subspecies and intergrades of a particular species. For example, members of the *Lampropeltis getula* complex include California kings, Florida kings, Mexican black kings, etc. All milk snakes belong to the *L. triangulum* complex. The *L. mexicana* complex is confusing in that it includes a number of snakes that are generally considered very closely related, yet some currently are considered true species rather than subspecies of *L. mexicana*, including *L. alterna* and *L. ruthveni*. The fourth complex would be the *L. calligaster* complex, which includes three subspecies of mole kingsnakes. They are called complexes because it is unlikely that all of the subspecies really do belong to the same species, but there is no consensus on how to split them up.

Most species of kingsnakes, including California kingsnakes, are crepuscular, meaning they are active at dawn and dusk.

under the threat of being eaten by predators or that are at the mercy of fluctuating environmental conditions. It is known that captive specimens of *Lampropeltis* can easily live for more than 15 years, with plenty of individuals recorded at over 20 years of age.

Human Impact on Wild Populations

As with most types of animals, the alteration of the land by the exploding human population is a direct threat to many types of reptiles. Many kingsnakes have adapted to utilizing piles of human debris for hiding spots and barns and agricultural areas for their abundance of rodents for food. However, humans do more harm than good to snakes and their habitat.

Countless snakes are killed when trying to cross roads that run through their habitat. For some species, habitat destruction has concentrated the last surviving members into small parcels of land. In addition, overcollection for the pet trade has nearly eliminated some species from their habitat. Still other people loathe snakes because of perpetuated misunderstandings and irrational fears and will kill any snake they encounter.

Fortunately, some species are protected in certain critical areas, while others are in need of protection before they disappear completely. Because of captive breeding efforts, most *Lampropeltis* species have become well established in the pet trade, eliminating the need to collect wild specimens. Going into the field and searching for snakes can be a fun experience, and collecting only their photographs and letting them go afterward can be much more rewarding than bringing the actual snake home.

Chapter 2

Kingsnakes As Pets

Before purchasing a kingsnake as a pet, first consider a number of things to make sure that a snake is the right choice for you and your family. You must understand all the requirements needed by your snake for proper health.

Important Questions

Here are a number of questions to ask yourself when considering the acquisition of a kingsnake for a pet.

Is It Legal for Me to Own a Snake in My Neighborhood?

As reptiles have become more popular as pets, more and more laws are being written to restrict ownership because of the actions of irresponsible owners and because many people still fear and misunderstand snakes. Certain states, counties, and cities may have their own laws governing the keeping of various types of reptiles. Some restrict ownership of any species, while others may not allow the keeping of native or certain exotic species. Familiarize yourself with current laws restricting reptile ownership in your area. Even if it is legal for you to keep a kingsnake or milk snake, homeowners' associations or landlords may not approve of these types of pets in areas under their jurisdiction. Breaking the law under these circumstances only makes things worse for responsible reptile keepers.

Will My Family Approve of a Snake in the House?

Although you may find snakes fascinating, many other people still have a strong dislike or irrational fear of snakes. Make sure that everyone living in your home approves of the presence of a snake. Some family members may be cautious of snakes for a number of reasons, usually based on myth and negative portrayal in the media and movies. Owning a snake can be an educational experience on many levels; ownership allows willing individuals to understand snakes better and respect them as an important part of the animal kingdom.

Will I Be Happy if My Snake Hides Much of the Time?

Many people like to have their reptiles on display where they can see them all the time. Unfortunately, kingsnakes prefer to hide most of the time and will not always be out in the open. They require dark hiding spaces to be happy in a captive environment. Do not selfishly neglect this necessity solely so that you can see your pet. Your snake may be stressed from feeling insecure, especially if it is kept in bright light or in a high-traffic area where people frequently walk by. If you want a reptile that will always be on display, kingsnakes do not make good choices.

Can I Provide the Proper Temperatures My Snake Requires?

Kingsnakes and milk snakes require fairly warm cage temperatures for a normal healthy life. You can provide this warmth by either purchasing special cage heating equipment with thermostats to regulate the temperature or by keeping the room at a proper temperature. Temperatures that get too low or too high will be harmful or fatal to your snake. If you plan to breed your snakes, provide a cooling period during the winter months, which may require additional cooling equipment in warmer areas. The only practical way to do this is to cool the entire room. If you are unable to invest in the equipment necessary for providing the correct temperatures, a kingsnake or milk snake may not be a good choice.

Do I Have Enough Space to Properly House My Snake?

Even though a hatchling kingsnake can be maintained in a small cage that takes up very little room, certain species may grow over 5 feet (1.5 m) long, requiring a suitably sized cage. Do not try to squeeze a snake this large in a small cage.

Will My Snake's Diet Be an Issue With the Family?

The most readily available food for kingsnakes is rodents. Rodents are available live and frozen. Frozen rodents are kept in the freezer until they are needed, at which point you must thaw them to room temperature prior to offering them to your snake. Unless you have a separate freezer for your frozen rodents, your family may not approve of dead mice in

Many states require permits to keep snakes, especially locally endangered types, such as Saint Helena Mountain kingsnakes.

the same freezer that you keep your food. Although securely bagged frozen rodents do not pose any contamination issues to nearby food, family members may still not like the idea.

Before you bring a snake home, make sure that no one in the house objects to its presence. An eastern milk snake is pictured.

Aside from frozen rodents, live rodents are another option for feeding your snake. Frozen rodents are preferable to live rodents, but some keepers may only have access to live rodents in their area. Even though it is a natural process, your family may not like the thought of mice being killed by your snake. Be sure to discuss this issue with your family and get everyone's approval before purchasing a kingsnake or milk snake.

Do I Have a Reliable Source of Food for My Snake?

Because snakes generally eat one rodent at least once a week, you will need to make sure that you have a steady source of properly sized mice available to you. If you don't have a local pet store that supplies frozen or live rodents, you can mail order them in bulk.

Will My Family Be Able to Safely Handle My Snake?

No snake ever should be considered completely tame. Even the most docile animal may suddenly bite without warning. Snakes may latch on to their owner's hand when feeling threatened or if they are expecting food. If you own a snake, expect to be bitten. A kingsnake bite can be painful and can draw blood, and often a kingsnake may clamp down on its owner's hand or other body part and not let go. This can be a very nerve-wracking experience for some. With time, you will learn your snake's behavior and know when it may be getting ready to bite.

Many kingsnakes can be acclimated to frequent handling and may seem tame, but always exercise caution. In general, milk snakes such as Pueblan milk snakes seem less likely to bite than kingsnake subspecies of *Lampropeltis getula* complex, but Pueblan milks are often known to move in very unpredictable jerky movements when unhappy. A variety of snake-handling tools such as hooks and tongs is available, but it is best not to use them because they can cause severe injury to snakes if improperly used.

Kingsnakes are notorious for their habit of expelling large amounts of feces and/or musk on the handler. This is a natural defensive tactic that usually happens with snakes that are not accustomed to handling or that are otherwise feeling threatened. Many people find this disgusting, and the smell of snake musk may not be easy to wash off. If you choose to own a kingsnake or milk snake, expect this to happen.

Another handling consideration is the possibility of contracting *Salmonella* bacteria from your pet. *Salmonella* causes an infection called salmonellosis (or just salmonella) that can cause from mild to severe and even life-threatening symptoms in humans. Anyone who handles a snake must be taught to immediately sanitize their hands afterward. Children must be supervised at all times. In addition, reptiles must be kept away from people with compromised immune systems, young children, and nursing mothers. Conscientious owners who practice good hygiene rarely contract salmonella, but it is a possibility of which everyone in the household needs to be aware.

Is Someone Available To Care for My Snake When I Am Away?

All pet owners struggle with the dilemma of finding a suitable pet sitter while traveling away from home. It is easier to find someone to take care of a dog or cat than it is a reptile. If you are a frequent traveler and don't have someone reliable and comfortable around snakes to take care of your pet, you may need to rethink the idea of having a snake as a pet.

Acquisition

If you have determined that a kingsnake or milk snake is the right pet for you and your family, you now must decide where you will obtain one. Also, you must decide whether to get a wild-caught or captive-bred snake.

Kingsnakes in the *getula* group, such as this desert kingsnake, may be more likely to bite than milk snakes.

Wild-Caught Snakes

It may be fun to catch your own snake as a pet. If you choose this route, first familiarize yourself with collecting laws in the area in which you choose to search. There may be state and local regulations

Choosing a Healthy Snake

When deciding upon a snake to purchase from a breeder or a pet store, look at several factors to determine whether it is healthy or not.

- Make sure that the entire snake appears healthy. There should be no pieces of shed skin adhering to the head, eyes, tail tip, or anywhere else. The snake should have a bright and glossy coloration. An exception would be if it was about to shed; at this time, the eyes and dark portions of the body will appear to be a cloudy blue-gray.

- Ask to hold the snake. A healthy animal will be active and try to escape your grasp, or it may become defensive and strike at you. A scared kingsnake or milk snake may often defecate on the handler, but this is a normal defense tactic. A tame individual may firmly wrap a portion of its body around a finger or wrist. Avoid snakes that feel limp or that have a "hollow" feel in their abdomen. A snake in hand should be holding its head up and act alert, and its body should feel firm and plump; the backbone should not visibly protrude.

- Inspect the snake more closely. Check the entire body, especially around the nostrils and eyes for the presence of tiny black round objects that may be parasitic mites. Check around the mouth for any signs of infection. Check the vent for caked feces or irritation. Gently run a finger down the snake's spine, and feel for any irregularities or kinks. Also, run your finger along the snake's underside to feel for any hard masses in the body.

- Inquire about what the snake has been eating, and ask if you can see it eat. Check the cage for evidence of fresh and healthy-looking feces, which indicate that it is eating. Liquefied or discolored feces are indicators of health problems. Healthy snake feces are brown with some white chalky material (the urates).

- Observe to see that the snake is being provided the proper environment. This includes proper temperature, clean bedding, fresh water, and a hiding place. Look around the enclosures of the other reptiles to see if they receive proper care.

Following this advice will help to ensure that the snake you select is a healthy one. If the snake is wild caught, you should also take it to a veterinarian for a health check. This is not a bad idea for a captive-bred snake either.

protecting the collection of snakes in certain areas. Certain species may be protected, while other more common types may be free for the taking.

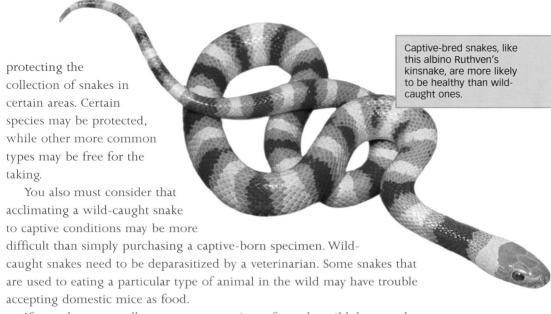

Captive-bred snakes, like this albino Ruthven's kinsnake, are more likely to be healthy than wild-caught ones.

You also must consider that acclimating a wild-caught snake to captive conditions may be more difficult than simply purchasing a captive-born specimen. Wild-caught snakes need to be deparasitized by a veterinarian. Some snakes that are used to eating a particular type of animal in the wild may have trouble accepting domestic mice as food.

If you choose to collect your own specimen from the wild, be sure that you can accurately identify both venomous and nonvenomous snakes native to the area. Some milk snakes closely resemble the highly venomous coral snake that may live in the same habitat. Do not handle any snake until you are positive of its identification.

Captive-Bred Snakes

Nearly every species of kingsnake and many species of milk snakes are successfully established in herpetoculture. The purchase of captive-bred snakes is preferable to purchasing wild-caught individuals. Captive-bred snakes will have fewer health problems due to low levels of parasites, and they have been adjusted to captive housing and feeding conditions since they were hatched. A much wider variety of colors and patterns are selectively bred in captivity for many species, often resulting in appearances that may be more desirable to some than the typical wild coloration.

The increasing availability of captive-produced snakes makes the collection of wild specimens unnecessary. Collecting pressures have greatly reduced the natural populations of many reptile species. Certain collecting practices, such as tearing open rotting logs in search of snakes, also destroys important habitats of other organisms in natural areas. Buying a captive-bred snake not only helps ensure that your new snake is healthy, it also reduces the degradation of natural habitats.

Don't Buy a Sick Snake

It may be tempting to buy an obviously sick snake in the hope of saving it, but don't do it. Purchasing an obviously sick kingsnake to rehabilitate it almost always ends badly. It is very difficult to rehabilitate a sick snake, especially for a hobbyist. Additionally, by purchasing a sick kingsnake, you have financially rewarded a vendor for mistreating his or her animals. It is better to pass on the snake, politely inform the vendor that the snake is sick, and take your business elsewhere.

Choosing the Right Species

Although most commonly available species of *Lampropeltis* can be kept under similar conditions, certain species may have distinct requirements. Some may tend to be more aggressive or difficult to handle, some may grow larger than others, and some may be more difficult to feed. Some species from dry areas may not do well in areas of high humidity, and those from high elevations may dislike hot summers. It is best to do research on the special requirements of each species before purchasing your snake. Individual species accounts are available elsewhere in this book.

Purchasing

When seeking your first kingsnake or milk snake, try to shop around if possible. Quality of health varies depending on the supplier and the conditions in which the snake was kept. If you buy from a pet shop, check to see that the staff has the proper knowledge to care for their reptiles. There are reputable pet shops with excellent reptile products and knowledge, and these are of course favorable sources for quality animals. Do your research to find the pet store that seems the most reptile savvy.

Aside from pet stores, many commercial and private reptile breeders provide quality animals. Some specialize in colubrids, such as kingsnakes and milk snakes, and they often offer a wider variety of colors and ages. Some breeders will sell their hatchlings fresh out of the egg to avoid having to take care of them, while other breeders prefer to "head start" their hatchlings, keeping them for several weeks before offering them for sale. This ensures that their animals are healthy and feeding, which is, of course, preferable to purchasing a freshly hatched snake. This is important with some species such as gray-banded kings, because initially they may be difficult to feed on pinky mice.

Another source for healthy snakes is one of the many reptile shows held at least annually in larger cities. Often, breeders will have a wide selection from which to choose, and they are usually willing to share helpful advice. Going to reptile shows is a convenient way to "shop around" with various vendors at the same time.

Still another source is the Internet, where many breeders have websites offering their current inventory, and some even have pictures of individual snakes, allowing the buyer to choose a specific one. In addition, serious hobbyists create many websites, and searching these sites often will provide good leads on reputable online sources for quality animals.

It's best not to handle a new snake for a few days so that it can settle in to its new surroundings. This is a gray-banded kingsnake.

If you order your snakes from a distant source, make sure that the seller is knowledgeable with shipping live reptiles properly. Shipping during the winter and summer months is tricky because the package containing the reptiles may be exposed to a variety of temperature extremes that can be fatal. Breeders use heat packs and cold packs during certain months, but even these can cause harm if not used properly. Hatchling snakes are normally shipped in plastic deli cups with ventilation holes punched in the sides. Adults are often shipped in pillowcases or similar cloth bags that are securely tied at the open end. These are packed in cardboard boxes insulated with foam inserts. Reptiles should only be shipped for overnight delivery and should never be in transit for longer than 24 hours.

Acclimation

When bringing home a newly purchased reptile, avoid handling it for several days so that the snake doesn't have to undergo additional stress. This also will allow your pet to get used to its new environment. Provide hiding places to make it feel more secure, and avoid any contact for a day or two.

If the snake was shipped to you, it has just gone through a very stressful experience during shipping. After a long time in transit, your new pet will be thirsty. When you finish unpacking your new snake, give it a water bowl. Avoid offering food for the first few days until it settles in.

Chapter 3

Housing

Most kingsnakes do not have complex caging requirements. As long as some basic needs are met, a very simple and easily maintained caging setup will work well for most of the commonly available species. That is not to say that a more complex, naturalistic setup is out of the question for the advanced keeper.

Types of Enclosures

There are many different options for housing your snake. Most will work equally well, so which one you use is mostly a matter of preference.

Glass and acrylic aquariums with secure-fitting lids are easily obtainable and affordable options that allow high visibility of the occupant.

Custom-made wood cages with a glass or acrylic viewing window in the front can be very attractive. All surfaces and corners of wood cages must be thoroughly sealed to allow for easy cleaning and to prevent moisture and waste from being absorbed into the wood. Custom cages also can be made out of sheets of melamine or PVC, which have nonporous surfaces that make cleaning very simple. Melamine cages must have the corners sealed with silicone caulking to prevent moisture from being absorbed into the wood core of the material, which will cause distortion of the cage.

Several companies manufacture molded plastic or fiberglass cages with glass fronts. There are many sizes, colors, and styles on the market, and many have places for lights and heating accessories. Many of these molded cages have detachable sliding glass panes that serve as both access doors and viewing windows. Sliding glass doors must be secured in some way to prevent larger snakes from working the doors open simply by rubbing against the glass.

Rack systems also are available that hold a varying number of cages. The cages are usually lidless plastic trays that slide out of the rack-like drawers. (The top of the shelf serves as the lid for the tray beneath it.) Several companies offer rack systems, or you can build your own rack out of melamine, PVC, or sealed plywood and use plastic storage bins with ventilation holes drilled in them. This type of setup is usually only practical for a serious breeder who is looking for a space-efficient method of housing a large collection. The trays usually are not transparent and therefore offer little in the way of viewing opportunity through the cage.

Many breeders use three sizes of plastic storage bins in their racks, commonly referred to (from smallest to largest) as "shoe boxes," "sweater boxes," and "blanket boxes." Sizes of

Cage Security

Regardless of the type of cage you choose, your pet must not be able to escape from it. Never underestimate the strength of your snake. Installing latches or locks to your cage door is the best way to prevent your snake from escaping. Snakes can squeeze through surprisingly small holes, so size ventilation holes accordingly.

Bureau-style rack systems are popular for housing larger snake collections because they can house many snakes in a small space.

these types of containers vary depending on the manufacturer, but shoe boxes are generally sized for hatchling snakes for their first year, at which point they can be moved up to a sweater box. Many of the smaller kingsnakes can comfortably live the rest of their lives in a sweater box. A blanket box is required for adults of the largest species. These types of containers are best used without a lid in a secure rack. Shoe boxes are generally the only size cage that can be used with the accompanying lid. Sweater box and blanket box lids usually do not have locking tabs that are secure enough to prevent even a subadult snake from pushing out with minimal effort. Even if they seem to be tight, do not underestimate the strength of your snake. The locking tabs usually are only present on the ends of the cage, and the lids are often flexible enough in between these tabs to allow a snake to squeeze through without unsnapping the lid.

In addition to shoe boxes, hatchling snakes also can be housed in small plastic "critter keepers" that are readily available at most pet stores. These are convenient options for housing a snake for its first several months before it outgrows the container.

Thoughts on Constructing Your Own Cage

Here are some things to need to keep in mind if you decide to build your own kingsnake cage:

- **Avoid metal window screens; snakes may rub their noses raw on the material.**
- **Do not allow rough or sharp edges of materials to be in contact with the snake's living quarters. Check the cage for projecting splinters and nails. Sharp edges of mesh must be concealed.**
- **All wooden surfaces must be thoroughly coated with several layers of polyurethane or a similar sealant. All corners must be caulked with a waterproof sealant.**
- **When constructing a cage, keep the interior as simple as possible to allow for easy cleaning.**
- **Make sure all lids or doors are secure and preferably latched or locked.**
- **Provide adequate ventilation.**

Cage Dimensions

When purchasing or building a cage for your snake, consider the amount of space it needs. Kingsnakes generally do not need very large amounts of space to be happy, yet you do not want to provide a cage that is too small, either. When determining the size of the cage, consider floor area and height. (Cage height is not usually important with most species of *Lampropeltis*, but it may be to the keeper, to allow for a better view in the cage.) Although some species will occasionally climb through the branches of low trees or shrubs, they are predominantly ground dwellers.

Floor surface area is the most important factor when deciding on the proper cage size. The minimum area required will be determined by the size of your snake. A hatchling requires a small enclosure. Never house a hatchling in an oversized cage. Although you may feel that a larger cage with more room for your snake to travel around is beneficial, a hatchling may never even utilize that much space. It may even have difficulty locating the water bowl or food in the seemingly vast expanse of cage floor space, which could result in dehydration or starvation. A hatchling will be perfectly happy in a cage with floor dimensions of about 1 square foot (900 square cm) or slightly less. As mentioned earlier, plastic "critter keepers" are good choices for housing hatchlings. Small aquariums will also

Young kingsnakes, such as this Sonoran mountain kingsnake, can be comfortably housed in shoebox- and sweaterbox-sized enclosures.

work, but avoid sizes larger than 10 gallons (38 l) for hatchlings.

As your snake grows, its cage size will need to be increased accordingly. A juvenile to subadult snake less than 24 inches (61 cm) long will be comfortable in a standard 10- to 15-gallon (37.9-56.8 l) aquarium or similarly sized cage. Any snake more than 24 inches (61 cm) long will require a greater amount of floor space. The largest kingsnakes will need a cage with at least 5 square feet (0.5 square m) of floor space, and a cage with as much as 12 square feet (1.1 square m) of floor space is not out of the question for a large kingsnake.

Substrate

You can use many materials to cover the floor of your snake's cage. A variety of commercially available substrates work well for snakes, while others are not recommended. When deciding upon a substrate, consider its cost, attractiveness, suitability for your snake, absorbency, and ease of cleaning. It should preferably be loose enough to allow for your snake to burrow in if it so chooses.

Wood Shavings

Aspen bedding, available either in shredded or chipped form, is a popular choice. It is absorbent, easy to spot clean, and attractive. If you provide a relatively thick layer, your snake may like to burrow in the aspen bedding. If some aspen bedding is accidentally ingested, it passes easily and won't cause internal impactions.

Other chipped or shredded wood products are available. Some keepers like the appearance of cypress mulch or pine bark nuggets, available at many garden centers. Be careful of products marked as cypress mulch "blends", which include a variety of other types of wood, including some that might be harmful to your snake. Avoid all wood products made from cedar, eucalyptus, or any other tree that has fragrant wood. Cedar chips are often sold as bedding for small pet mammals, but the phenols in cedar wood are toxic to reptiles.

Most kingsnakes, such as this baby albino prairie king, can be housed safely on aspen shavings.

Recycled Paper Bedding

Several companies offer substrates made of recycled paper products. These materials are safe, absorbent, easy to burrow in, and make cleaning simple, but they don't have a very natural look. Nonetheless, shredded paper substrates are an excellent choice for snakes.

Newspaper

Many keepers prefer newspaper as a safe, cheap, and effective substrate. Use several layers to increase the absorbency. Snakes often will prefer to hide under the newspaper, and may move the paper around the cage if it is not secured to the floor of the cage in some way.

Naturalistic Substrates

For an even more natural look, some keepers like to use dried leaves that are collected from an area known to be free of pesticides. It is best to bake leaves used as substrate in an oven set at 200°F (93.3°C) for about 15 minutes to kill any parasites that may be hiding in them.

The use of sand as a substrate in a naturalistic setup for desert-dwelling species is controversial. While some claim that sand will result in intestinal impactions, others have maintained snakes on sand for years without any problems. In the wild, snakes often ingest sand, leaves, and other foreign objects accidentally in the course of swallowing their prey, and these materials are normally passed through the body without any ill effects. If a captive snake is unable to pass these materials, it may be due to other husbandry issues that are compromising the snake's health. Even so, it's best to avoid large, granular substrates like gravel (including aquarium gravel), ground corncobs, orchid bark, etc., that might be large enough to cause an impaction if swallowed.

A safer and commercially available alternative to sand is calcium carbonate-based sand made specifically for use as a caging substrate. It comes in many colors, including some that mimic the variety of hues present in desert sands. Calcium carbonate is safer for ingestion than other sands, such as those derived from quartz or granite, because the snake can easily absorb it.

Paper towels and newspaper are economical substrate choices, but they must be cleaned frequently.

Light

Light is apparently not important for the health of kingsnakes. Some reptiles, such as iguanas, require natural sunlight or an artificial lighting with similar spectral output for proper nutrition, but snakes in general do not seem to suffer any nutritional problems from lack of exposure to sunlight. In the wild, kingsnakes bask in the sunlight, but this is normally done at times when the snakes need to raise their body temperature, often in the morning following a cool night. That is not to say that exposure to ultraviolet light during that time isn't beneficial to snakes in some way, but this has not yet been proven. Plenty of success in the captive care and breeding of kingsnakes over many years seems to show that ultraviolet light is not critical to their health.

Light still can be used in an enclosure for either heating or viewing your pet. Because kingsnakes generally shun bright light unless they need to bask for warmth, you must provide suitable dark hiding spaces in the cage where they it can retire if it wants to. Never deny a snake a hiding spot just so that you can selfishly see it at all times. Forcing it to live exposed under bright lights may be very stressful for your pet and result in greater susceptibility to other health problems.

The type of light you use will depend on your caging setup. Keep in mind that an incandescent bulb produces much more heat than a fluorescent tube. Heat produced from a lightbulb may be desirable in some situations as long as the temperature is not allowed to get too hot. Experiment carefully, and monitor your snake's cage temperature closely. There are many different types of fluorescent tubes available that vary by their spectral output.

One Per Cage

It is always best to house kingsnakes individually. Many kingsnakes may decide to eat their cagemate, even if it is nearly the same size. A male and female may be housed together temporarily for breeding purposes, but otherwise they should be separated soon after copulation ends. Kingsnakes will readily eat other species of snakes, as well as lizards and amphibians, so do not mix species. Even if they don't eat their cagemate, feeding presents problems, especially if both snakes latch on to the same food item. If you plan to have multiple snakes, be prepared to devote the space so that they can be housed individually.

Generally, those with a spectrum as close as possible to natural sunlight bring out the best appearance of your snake and its enclosure.

Temperature and Heating

It is up to you to provide the proper temperatures necessary for your snake. Heating needs may vary somewhat depending on the species you keep. If you intend to breed your snakes, both heating and cooling are critical for best results. Exposing your snake to temperatures that are either too hot or too cold can be harmful or fatal to your pet.

Temperatures and Thermal Gradients

The only way that reptiles can regulate their body temperature is by allowing the environment to warm or cool their bodies. Snakes seek out warm spots or bask in the sun if they are too cold and then retire in a shady spot or other cooler locality when they get too hot. To re-create this in captivity, many keepers choose to offer a hot spot on one side of the cage and a cool spot on the opposite side. If done properly, there will be a gradual temperature change across the length of the cage, from warm to cool. This thermal gradient will allow your snake to decide at what temperature it wants to be at any given time.

To create a temperature gradient, orient a heat source on one side of the cage. Experimentation is necessary *before* the snake is housed in the cage. With the heat source running, monitor the temperatures on both sides of the cage using thermometers. An infrared temperature gun, which accurately reads surface temperatures, is an even better investment for a keeper of a large collection of reptiles. Most temperature guns have a feature that allows you to scan from one side of the cage to the other to instantly see the change in temperature.

Various factors such as cage construction, ventilation, ambient room temperature, and substrate can affect the creation of a smooth temperature gradient. If using an undertank heat source, the type of substrate and depth may affect how much heat is transferred. For most species, the maximum temperature of the hot spot should be in the 85° to 88°F (29.4° to 31.1°C) range, while the coolest spot should be 70° to 75°F (21.1° to 24°C). The average temperature between the hot and cool spots should optimally be between 78° and 80°F (25.6° and 26.7°C).

Other keepers successfully keep kingsnakes without offering a thermal gradient. With a few exceptions, most kingsnakes can be successfully kept at a temperature of 80°F (26.7°C) year round if they are not going to be bred. This is best done by heating the whole room in winter and cooling the room in the summer with an air conditioner. Using this method, no additional heating equipment is necessary. A variety of thermostats are available that can be plugged into room heaters so that they can be automatically turned on if the room temperature gets too cold.

Keepers with rack systems often use heat tape to keep their snakes at the proper temperature.

Never allow your snake to be exposed to high temperatures for long periods of time. Continuous exposure to temperatures in the upper 80s or higher (30.5°C or more) can be harmful or fatal. Though many kingsnakes originate from hot desert habitats, don't assume they are tolerant of hot temperatures. They will never be found active during the heat of the day and will only emerge from their cool subterranean recesses when the outside temperature cools in the evenings.

Heating Methods

There are several options when it comes to cage heating. When choosing your heating method, stick with types that are fixed to the outside of the cage. Avoid products that require power cords or other electrical components inside the cage where your snake can come in contact with them or where they may get wet.

Several styles of undertank heating pads are manufactured specifically for use with reptiles. These are best used under one end of glass or acrylic aquariums or plastic cages such as shoeboxes and sweater boxes. Similarly, heat tapes or heat cables are available in different lengths and can be run under the ends of a number of cages that are placed next to each other.

These heating products must be used in conjunction with a reliable thermostat, several of which are available specifically for use with reptiles. Always verify that your heating system works properly before you add your snakes to their cages. Install a thermometer in your snake's cage, and always check to make sure everything is working properly at least once a day when using these types of systems. Thermostat malfunctions do occur, and there have been reports of fires, cooked animals, etc. from malfunctioning or improperly used heat sources.

Lighting as a Heat Source

As mentioned in the section on lighting, certain types of bulbs, such as the inexpensive incandescent bulbs, can be used as a method for heating an enclosure. These should be located outside of the cage, shining through a metal screen or hardware cloth lid. Some molded plastic or fiberglass cages have built-in recesses to house

Sonoran mountain kingsnakes and other species that originate at high altitudes require slightly cooler temperatures than more common types.

light fixtures. Never install a light fixture inside a cage where a snake can come in contact with the hot bulb or electrical components. A light that is being used as a heat source should be located at one end of the cage to create the proper temperature gradient.

Other than the readily available incandescent bulb, there are specialty basking lights made for use with reptiles. Still another alternative are ceramic heating elements that screw into standard incandescent fixtures. These do not emit light but can be placed over a cage in a similar fashion to a light.

Humidity

Humidity requirements will vary depending on the species you keep. Those species from dry habitats will not like the amount of humidity you would provide to those from wetter habitats. Regardless of habitat, your snake will also benefit from higher amounts of humidity in its cage when it is about to shed. For raising humidity in a cage, you could simply increase the size of the water bowl. Misting the insides of the cage also will quickly increase the humidity within the cage. Avoid making the cage too wet. The substrate should never remain damp for extended periods of time. Using substrates such as cypress mulch will help retain moisture that will contribute to the humidity within the cage, but will remain dry enough that it won't result in the skin infections that develop when a snake is kept on wet substrate. It is always best to keep your snake's cage on the dry side, and adjust only if you begin to see shedding problems.

Hide Spots

Hiding spots should always be present for your snake. This is especially important in brightly lit enclosures. In cages with a temperature gradient, at least three hiding spots

Hot Rocks

Despite safer alternatives, products commonly referred to as hot rocks are unfortunately still available in many pet stores. These fake stones with built-in heating element are meant to be used inside the cage as heat source. The problem with these products is that they do not offer any type of temperature gradient. Snakes are either forced to expose themselves to the scorching temperatures of the hot rock or be too cold. Severe burns have been attributed to snakes trying to keep warm by remaining in constant contact with hot rocks. Since there are safer choices readily available, avoid using hot rocks.

should be provided: one in the cool zone, one in the hot zone, and one in the middle zone. Hiding spots can be as simple as a cardboard box that can be disposed of when dirty and replaced with another. A plastic saucer normally used under plant pots can work well when a suitable sized hole is drilled in the center and placed in the cage upside down. Many easily obtainable items can be modified into hiding spots. There are even commercially available plastic hiding places you can purchase at a pet shop.

It is best that a hiding spot allows the animal to fit in it with very little additional space. Snakes feel most secure when their bodies are in contact with their surroundings on nearly all sides. You will be surprised at what your snake will be able to fit its entire body into. With this in mind, do not use something that you can not open easily to retrieve your snake or thoroughly clean out.

A thick layer of loose substrate, such as shredded or chipped aspen bedding may be used by your snake to burrow and hide in. A snake may also choose to feel even more secure under a flat object, such as a section of wood or bark placed on top of the substrate.

More natural-looking hiding spots can also serve as caging decorations. Curved or hollow sections of cork bark are available at pet stores and are durable and decorative. A thick layer of clean, pesticide free leaves can add a natural look and provide a secure place

No matter what type of cage you use, you must provide your kingsnake with a few hiding spots.

for your snake to burrow in. Another natural material that make good hiding spots are large rigid dead fan palm leaves (with the spiny leaf stem removed).

Stacked rocks should not be used for making hiding spots. The movements of your snake will shift the rocks, causing them to collapse and possibly kill your snake. If you create a hiding area out of stacked rocks, they must be epoxied into a fixed position to prevent accidents.

Water

Clean drinking water must be present at all times. A heavy, secure bowl that can not be tipped or easily moved around is best. Ceramic crocks work best for larger snakes and are available in several sizes. Small deli cups work well for hatchlings. Your snake may choose to soak in its water bowl when it is about to shed. Keep this in mind when selecting the size the bowl. Have a bowl large enough that it can almost completely submerge itself yet excess water will not be displaced onto the cage substrate.

Water quality should be taken into consideration when choosing the type of water you offer your snake. If you wouldn't drink the water, don't offer it to your snake. If your tap water is of poor quality, it might be best to purchase purified bottled water from your grocery store. Many keepers have used city drinking water with chlorine and other chemical additives for long periods of time without ill effects on their snakes, but water quality varies in different regions. If you have a choice, it is best to opt for better quality water whenever possible.

Other Cage Furnishings

Other decorative objects can be added to your snake's cage to improve its appearance and even serve your pet. Natural objects such as driftwood, branches, and rocks add interest to the viewer, while serving as additional structures to make your snake feel secure, or simply to rub against to help in the shedding process. Though most kingsnakes are not considered arboreal, they will utilize branches in their enclosure, and may even thermoregulate by moving up or down branches if they are placed under an overhead heat lamp. Additional objects that add to the overall surface area within the cage surely give a snake more opportunities for exercise than a sterile cage with just the bare necessities.

As mentioned earlier, heavy objects such as rocks used in cages can be hazardous if not situated securely. Your snake is stronger than you think and will be able to move around rocks of considerable size. Avoid stacking rocks. Position them so they will not roll or tip over. Do not rest rocks on top of the substrate. A burrowing snake may crawl under them and shift the rock, potentially crushing the snake or breaking the cage glass. To avoid this,

Driftwood, artificial plants, and other decorations make a kingsnake cage more interesting for both the keeper and the snake.

make sure the rock is resting directly on the bottom of the cage under the substrate.

Plants

Potted plants can be used for a variety of purposes. Aside from being a natural decoration, plants with the appropriate type of foliage can serve as hiding spots, and the regular watering required by the plant will help with humidity maintenance. Plants should be types that are sturdy, and not easily crushed or matted down by your snake. Choosing plants to accompany large snakes is more challenging than for small snakes. Plants are best kept in pots. Vining tropical plants with large leaves such as pothos (Epipremnum aureum), philodendrons (Philodendron sp.), and arrowhead plants (Syngonium sp.) are commonly available as house plants and are somewhat resistant to being matted down by larger snakes. Their foliage also hangs downward, which conceals the pot. Two identical plants can also be purchased, and if one is flattened by your snake, it can be removed to be pruned back and recover while the second plant takes its place in the cage.

Cacti and succulents can be used in a desert setup with pleasing results, but make sure to use types that will not be crushed or broken by the movements of your snake. A snake's skin is resistant to cactus spines that would otherwise be very uncomfortable for people, so you don't need to worry about any resulting injuries. These plants are also best kept in pots, which can be sunken down in a thick layer of substrate or hidden behind rocks.

Cage Maintenance Schedule

In order to maintain the health of your pets as well as an attractive display, you will need to follow a regular maintenance schedule. The one presented here is a general guideline and some tasks may need to be done more frequently as needed.

Daily:
- Check drinking water level in water bowl. Make sure there are no feces, shed skin, substrate, scum, or any other material in the bowl. If there is, thoroughly clean the water bowl and refill with fresh water. If you would not want to drink it, your snake shouldn't drink it.
- Check the cage for feces, shed skin, and uneaten or regurgitated food items and spot clean as needed. If using newspaper on the floor of the cage, replace soiled paper.
- Check cage temperature. If providing a temperature gradient, check temperatures on the warm and cool side of the enclosure. Check thermostats and heating equipment to make sure everything is working properly.
- Inspect your snake for any problems, such as shedding difficulty, retained eyecaps, injuries, etc. and treat as necessary.
- Make sure cage doors are properly locked and secured.

Weekly:
- If using a newspaper substrate, replace it.
- Clean cage accessories, such as branches and hide boxes.
- Thoroughly sanitize water bowl if not changed since the previous week.

Every Month:
- Completely break down cage and sanitize all surfaces thoroughly.
- Completely replace substrate.

Live plants will require adequate lighting to look their best. Fluorescent lights are best for this purpose. Desert plants will require greater amount of light than most tropical foliage plants. Remember to monitor cage temperature when increasing the amount of light you have on a cage. Do not use any fertilizers or pesticides on plants contained within your snake's enclosure.

A simpler alternative to live plants are fake plants. A variety of silk or plastic plants are available, and many can look very realistic.

Some keepers may want to create a very naturalistic vivarium replicating the habitat their snake is from using plants and other items that would be found in their native range. This requires a lot of research, and plants from your snake's habitat may be difficult to locate or may otherwise be unsuitable for use in a vivarium. In many cases it can be done effectively, but these types of cages are often more difficult to maintain being that they can't be broken down and cleaned as easily. Live plants are not always necessary, and naturalistic setups can be made using things like specially selected rocks, dried leaves, branches, dried grass clumps, etc.

Cage Maintenance

A regular cage maintenance schedule should be followed to keep the habitat clean. Dirty conditions combined with humidity leads to a very unsanitary environment, which can directly affect your snake's health.

Remove shed skins and other wastes from the cage as soon as you see them.

King & Milk Snakes

Disinfectants for Cleaning Enclosures

Though there are many cleaning chemicals on the market, some may be unsuitable for use in reptile cages. Avoid any scented chemicals, such as pine scent and lemon scent. These can be toxic or irritating to reptiles. Dish soap mixed with warm water should be used for the initial cleaning of cages and supplies. Thoroughly rinse all soap residues away with warm water.

Household bleach is one of the best chemicals for sanitizing reptile cages. You will need to dilute it; add about one cup (0.2 l) of bleach to one gallon (3.8 l) of water. After a thorough cleaning with soapy water and rinsing, soak all non-porous cage materials such as water dishes in this diluted bleach for at least 15 minutes, and then rinse any residue off thoroughly and dry.

Disinfecting with bleach will not kill all parasites that can harm your snake. Ammonia is effective on other parasites not killed by bleach, including *Cryptosporidium*. After disinfecting with bleach, thoroughly rinse and dry all cage surfaces and supplies, and soak or wipe down with undiluted ammonia. Never mix ammonia and bleach together.

Always use bleach and ammonia in a well-ventilated area. It is recommended to wear rubber gloves, eye protection, and a respirator with chemical filters when working with these chemicals. Always rinse any chemicals off cages and supplies and allow to thoroughly dry before putting your animal back in its cage.

The floor of the cage should be cleaned any time fecal material is present. If you are using newspaper, change the entire cage. Feces can be manually spot-cleaned out of loose substrates such as chipped or shredded wood bedding. The walls of the cage should be cleaned as needed. Scrubbing with a damp towel will work well. Do not use cleaning chemicals inside the cage with animals. Clean water must always be available. When dirty, thoroughly wash the water bowl and replace with fresh water. If live potted plants are used, they should be removed and any fecal matter gently washed off. Artificial plants can be cleaned as well.

Once a month, break down your snake's cage and thoroughly cleanse all surfaces. Replace the substrate at this time.

Chapter 4

Feeding and Nutrition

As mentioned earlier in this book, kingsnakes earned their name from the fact that they regularly consume other snakes, including individuals of the same species. Aside from this cannibalistic urge, many species also eat just about any type of vertebrate they can capture and swallow, including birds, lizards, frogs, rodents, and other small mammals. Some species have more refined tastes, especially those with limited types of prey items in their natural habitat.

No Supplements Needed

Keepers of reptiles other than snakes know that vitamin/mineral supplementation is a crucial addition to their pet's diet. Some reptiles also require exposure to natural sunlight or an artificial lighting substitute to properly synthesize vitamin D3. Captive snakes normally will not need any supplementation to their diet if they are fed whole animals, such as rodents. They will get everything they need from various parts of the rodent's body.

When purchasing your snake from a reptile breeder or pet store, ask the staff what your potential choice has been eating under their care. Familiarize yourself with the feeding preferences of the species you are interested in before visiting a pet store. Some stores may not offer the proper diet to a snake. If you are buying a hatchling, make sure that it has been fed at least one meal. Hatchlings don't usually eat until a week or two after hatching, living on yolk reserves within their body for that time. Check its cage for feces, which indicate that it is eating. Buy a hatchling that is at least a month old so that you can easily tell it is eating and otherwise appears healthy.

Feeding Response

Feeding snakes can result in injury to the keeper. After a feeding routine is developed, a snake soon begins to sense the smell of food in the room before it is even in the cage. It learns where the door to the cage is and may anxiously wait for the door to open. As soon as the door opens, the snake may instantly and blindly strike out toward the source of the smell and may latch onto the person's hand instead of the food. Even without the smell of food in the room, a snake may learn to expect food any time the cage is opened and may strike out toward the owner. This reaction of immediately striking when the cage is opened is known as a "feeding response."

Many kingsnakes are voracious feeders and develop a feeding response that can be unnerving for the keeper, often shooting their entire body out of the cage with their mouth open in attempt to grab hold of something. If the keeper is not careful, the snake could bite down on his hand or another part of the body that is within reach. Certain species of kingsnakes often will clamp down on their owner's finger, refusing to let go. This can be scary and painful because all the snake's teeth are plunged into the flesh. The snake's mouth is not easy to pry open for removal. If it bites down on a fingertip, it often will begin swallowing the finger, much to the horror of the keeper!

Most of the kingsnakes, including California kingsnakes, are generalist feeders, eating the birds, snakes, lizards, and mammals that share their habitat.

Many owners panic in such a situation, shaking and hitting the snake and doing other things out of desperation that can injure it. Even though the bite may hurt, remain calm. Moving the part of the body in the snake's grasp will only make it bite down harder, thinking its prey is struggling. Remember, the snake is not intentionally trying to be malicious toward you; its reptilian brain thinks it has just captured food. Do not try to pry the snake's mouth open.

One method that *sometimes* works for getting a snake to let go is to hold it under some cool running water. Another method that *always* works is to hold the mouth of an open container of isopropyl alcohol next to the snake's mouth, squeezing the container to send alcohol vapors into its sensory organs. All snakes are irritated at the smell of alcohol and will instantly let go. Never allow any alcohol to come in contact with the snake's mouth, though. As soon as it lets go, it may still have the drive to eat and could immediately latch on to another finger unless its head is restrained and returned to its cage. Immediately clean the bite with an antiseptic, and use tweezers to remove any broken-off teeth that are embedded in your skin.

To avoid feeding response-related injuries, learn your snake's habits. Always be ready when opening the cage, even if your snake appears inactive. Use long tongs when offering

Kingsnakes do not crush their prey; they tighten their coils until it cannot breathe. Here, a wild California mountain kingsnake subdues a mouse.

food. Aside from your hands, keep all parts of your body away from the cage, especially your face.

Constriction and Swallowing

After your snake has its prey in its mouth, it will throw a few loops of its body around the item and constrict it in an attempt to kill it. It does not crush its prey to death but rather squeezes it so that it cannot breathe. Even if you offer dead prey, a snake often will still instinctively constrict its prey. This process lasts for a minute or two.

After the prey is dead (or in the case of pre-killed prey, when the snake realizes that the prey is dead), the swallowing process begins. The snake will normally seek out the head of the prey and begin swallowing it head first. Occasionally, the snake may decide to swallow it tail first. This will only become a problem on oversized prey, at which point the snake will regurgitate it and may or may not decide to make another attempt.

A snake's entire skull comprises a number of bones loosely connected together to allow for the expansion necessary to swallow oversized items. The snake's lower jaws dislocate to enable it to swallow prey that is wider than the diameter of the snake's head. During the swallowing process, the its head and mouth may appear crooked and bent in unnatural directions. This is normal, and after the meal is swallowed, the snake may repeatedly open and close its mouth in an attempt to relocate its jaws back into the proper place. The snake will slowly move the prey down the neck to the stomach using muscular undulations.

After feeding, your snake will want to retire to a hiding spot. Avoid disturbing it for at least a day after feeding. Handling your snake after feeding may cause it to regurgitate the food. Always feed it when cage temperatures are adequate. The temperature must remain warm enough for the rest of the week to allow digestion to take place. If the cage temperature is too cool, the food item will not be digested and will begin decomposing inside the snake, at which point it will regurgitate the food and possibly become ill.

Rodent Diet

Feeding exclusively rodents to your snake is probably the best and most convenient option. All species of kingsnakes eat mice or rats. Even picky species that prefer to eat lizards in the wild can be trained to accept rodents with a little effort. Rats and mice are readily available at pet stores that specialize in reptiles, and they are a nutritionally complete meal. Although you can purchase rodents live, many stores offer them pre-killed and frozen in bags. If you don't have a supplier in your area, or if you are maintaining a large collection of reptiles, you also can order frozen rodents from many different companies online or in reptile magazine advertisements. Still another option is to breed your own rodents.

Feeding Live Rodents

Offering live food creates the possibility of injury and even death to your snake. Once it has latched on to the mouse and begins to constrict it, the mouse will bite the snake in defense if it has a chance. Obviously, snakes in the wild have to deal with this on a regular basis, and they normally heal quickly from mouse bites without any need for treatment. Bites to the head can be a different story, because these areas become infected more often than other parts of the body when

The elastic skin of a kingsnake's neck and the flexible joints of its skull allow it to swallow larger prey.

bitten. Sometimes they heal without incident, but often they become severely infected and require veterinary treatment. If a mouse should happen to puncture your snake's eye, it requires veterinary treatment.

Never leave a live mouse in a snake's cage for more than a few hours. An uneaten live mouse left for long periods of time often will become desperate for food and attempt to eat the snake. You may be surprised to learn that a mouse could overpower a snake, but the snake eventually becomes so exhausted from escaping the mouse that it has no choice but to let the mouse begin gnawing on it. These injuries can be severe, with massive amounts of tissue loss or even death of the snake before you notice a problem. Avoid this situation by frequently checking on the cage and removing the uneaten mouse after a few hours. Often, this problem is the result of the keeper not thoroughly checking the cage for an uneaten mouse. Be sure to look behind the water bowl and cage decorations, as well as inside hiding spots.

Even if an uneaten live mouse doesn't decide to attack your snake, it still may cause damage to the snake's cage and furnishings. A rodent's powerful incisors can easily chew through plastic, wood, and other materials used to build cages, often

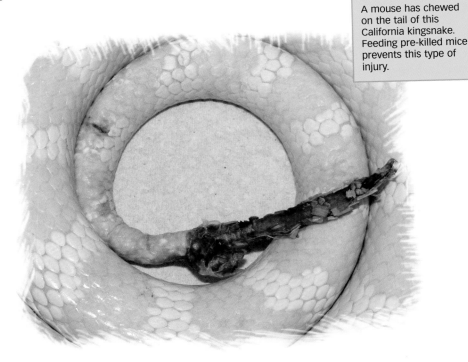

A mouse has chewed on the tail of this California kingsnake. Feeding pre-killed mice prevents this type of injury.

starting at a ventilation hole and gnawing at it until it is large enough that it (and your snake) can escape. In addition, mice may chew on electrical wires running to a heat source inside the cage, creating the danger of shock or fire.

If live rodents are the only snake food available in your area, the best course of action is to humanely pre-kill them before feeding them to your snake.

Feeding Thawed Frozen Rodents

Although a responsible keeper can feed live rodents and avoid the previously mentioned problems, thawed frozen rodents are a much simpler alternative. They are readily available at most pet stores that specialize in reptiles, or you can order them in bulk from various sources. Other members of the family may be disgusted at the thought of dead mice in the freezer next to the ice cream, so have another small freezer on hand if this is an issue.

If you choose to order frozen rodents from a distant source, talk to other reptile keepers and get their opinions on their preferred supplier. Aside from price (including shipping), you want to look for someone who provides mice that are clean and healthy, that

Thawing and Offering Frozen Rodents

Frozen rodents are best thawed over several hours at room temperature. Do not try to speed up the process by microwaving or exposing them to any other heat source. Thawing can be sped up by putting the frozen rodents in a resealable bag and submerging it into a container of warm—not hot—water. Only offer a thawed frozen rodent when it is at room temperature all the way through. Otherwise, your snake could regurgitate it because the snake's body is unable to raise the temperature. A thawed rodent may be fairly wet, so place the food on a dish or piece of paper so that the substrate does not stick to it and in turn become ingested by the snake.

were humanely euthanized, and that were fed a nutritious diet, such as lab blocks. Make sure that the mice are bagged in a sensible manner. Some careless rodent breeders will pack a bag full of pre-killed mice and then freeze them, resulting in a solid block of interlocking frozen mice. To extract one mouse, the entire block must be thawed. If the supplier bags multiple rodents together, make sure that it freezes the rodents first and then bags them. This way, individual rodents will be loose in the bag.

What Size Rodent to Feed?

Both mice and rats are usually sold in a variety of sizes. Different suppliers may have different names for different growth stages or sizes. One supplier's "medium" mouse may be larger or smaller on average than what another supplier considers to be medium. Most rodent breeders know that the average weight in grams of their

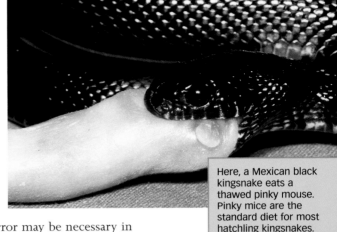

Here, a Mexican black kingsnake eats a thawed pinky mouse. Pinky mice are the standard diet for most hatchling kingsnakes.

various sizes, and some trial and error may be necessary in familiarizing yourself with their sizes. It is always easier to select your food items in person whenever possible.

As for juvenile rodent sizes, most breeders agree that newborn rodents of about a day old are called "reds," while those slightly older and a little larger are called "pinks" or "pinkies." Once hair begins to develop, they become known as "peach fuzzies" and then turn into "fuzzies" or "pups" when they get a full coat of hair yet are still nursing. After the fuzzy stage, they begin eating solid food, their eyes open, and the rodents begin to resemble smaller versions of adults. With mice, most suppliers refer to this size as "hoppers" or "weanlings," and anything larger than a hopper will often be called "medium" or "large" or "adult." The largest mice usually available are "retired breeders," which are old breeder mice that have been culled from a breeding colony due to productivity reduction resulting from old age.

With rats, breeders call the next size up from a fuzzy a "pup," and from there, "smalls," "mediums," "larges," and "jumbos" or "retired breeders." Some breeders even offer additional sizes such as "small-medium" and "medium-large." With nearly all species of kingsnakes, mice from pinks to adults are usually the primary food item, with small rats used on the largest individuals.

How do you know what size rodent to feed your snake? Hatchling kingsnakes normally require a newborn or "red" mouse. Obviously, as your snake grows, you will increase the food size. It is well known that many snakes can engulf prey that is seemingly too large, resulting in a noticeable bulge in the snake's midsection. A snake is able to temporarily dislocate specialized joints in its skull and jaws to aid in swallowing such a large meal, but that does not mean that it is good to regularly offer rodents that are at the upper size limit of your snake's abilities. The best rule of thumb is to offer a rodent that is about the same diameter as your snake's midsection. When swallowed, little to no bulge should be apparent in its body.

How Often To Feed?

Your snake's feeding schedule will be determined by several factors. A nonbreeding kingsnake or milk snake will be perfectly happy with an appropriately sized rodent once a week. On the other hand, a breeding female snake needs a significant amount of food through the duration of the breeding season. Some breeders feed their females almost daily during the breeding season. Breeder males require less food, with two meals per week perfectly adequate. Juvenile snakes will grow more quickly if fed more frequently, but many herpetoculturists frown upon "pushing" snakes to reach sexual maturity in a short period of time. Like nonbreeding adults, hatchlings are best fed at least once a week.

In the wild, snakes rarely are lucky enough to find a meal once a week. A snake may go weeks or even months without eating until it is finally lucky enough to capture something. Don't worry if your snake refuses its weekly meal. An upcoming shed may cause a snake to lose its appetite until the skin finally sheds. Assuming all of your snake's needs are being met (proper temperature, humidity, available hiding areas, etc), it should eat at the next offering. If your snake still won't eat after several attempts, take it to your reptile vet to see what the problem might be.

Alternatives to Rodents

Although kingsnakes eat a variety of vertebrates in the wild, avoid feeding other types of animals to your snake, especially if they are collected from the wild. Every wild animal has parasites, and you don't want your snake to become infected with something it obtained from its food.

Some manufacturers offer "sausages" specifically made to be fed to snakes and other reptiles as an alternative to using whole rodents or other animals for food. These sausages are filled with beef and/or poultry products, as well as other nutritional additives, and family members are often more open to having these kept in the freezer as opposed to dead rodents. The manufacturers claim that their products are nutritionally complete and require no additional vitamin or mineral supplementation. They are kept frozen until ready for use, at which point they are thoroughly thawed to room temperature.

Opinions vary on the use of these products. Some keepers have no problems getting their snake to eat sausages, while others do. It seems to be up to the snake's individual preference. It is difficult to transition a rodent-feeding snake to eating sausages, and you may have to rub the scent of a mouse on the sausages to help with the transition. Hatchlings often will refuse sausages as their first meal, and you may have to start them on newborn mice

Adult *Lampropeltis* should be fed about once a week. A Mexican milk snake is shown here.

and transition them to sausages after that point. Some snakes never seem to transition to eating sausages, so this feeding method is impractical for someone who maintains a larger collection of snakes and can't cater to each snake's individual food preferences. The sausages also tend to be more expensive than similarly sized rodents, so that is another factor to consider.

Problem Feeders

The only time that you may need to feed a wild-collected food item (such as a lizard) to your snake would be as a last resort with a stubborn feeder. Certain species of kingsnakes have natural food preferences other than rodents. This is a problem with some wild-collected species, but even captive-hatched examples of these species may refuse pinky mice and starve unless their needs are met. Often, these hatchlings can be coaxed to eat if offered a small lizard or a pinky mouse scented with a lizard. If you are concerned with the potential health risks that your snake may experience from eating wild prey items, consider freezing the food to kill any parasites.

Braining

Before resorting to feeding lizards, there is one method that sometimes works for getting nonfeeding hatchlings to eat. Pick a small, pre-killed newborn mouse and slice open its head to expose the brain. This gruesome method, known as "braining," often has surprising results, although this method is unsuitable for the squeamish. For some reason, the scent of the brain is appetizing to snakes that otherwise refuse to start out with unbrained pinks. If your snake refuses to eat brained pinks, try offering a lizard or lizard-scented pink.

Scenting

Lizards of the genus *Sceloporus*, which include fence lizards and swifts, can be collected from many parts of the United States. These species are the preferred food of many stubborn feeders, especially gray-banded kingsnakes. If you can't collect them in your area, you might be able to have a pet store order some from one of its sources. Any species, including those not native to your snake's natural range, seem to work. If you can't locate a *Sceloporus*, the next best choice is a green anole (*Anolis carolinensis*) or brown anole (*Anolis sagrei*), both readily available at most pet stores that carry reptiles. In a pinch, you can try any small lizard, but these two generally work best.

Baby *Sceloporus* or *Anolis* small enough to feed to a stubborn hatchling are not easy to find in the pet trade. If you only have larger anoles or swifts available, your first step should be to scent a tiny thawed frozen newborn pinky (red) mouse with the lizard. After thawing the red, wash it with a little soap to remove as much mouse scent as possible. Rinse the soap off and blot it dry with some paper towels. Next, gently rub all surfaces of the red on the lizard and offer the red to your snake.

If your snake accepts a lizard-scented newborn mouse, continue scenting its food a few more times, and then begin to offer unscented pinks. Often, the transition from scented to

No, They Don't Eat Crickets

Do not feed invertebrates such as insects and worms to kingsnakes. Aside from not being a part of their natural diet, invertebrates may cause serious digestive complications.

Unfortunately, pet stores that don't specialize in reptiles or that have an uneducated staff sometimes offer a noninsectivorous hatchling snake things like crickets or mealworms for food in their stores. Be wary of pet stores that have been offering their snakes insects, even if they insist that the snake is eating the insect—unless the snake is truly an insectivore, such as a rough green snake.

unscented pinks can be done easily after your snake recognizes pinkies as food. You can also try wrapping the red or pinkie in some shed lizard skin if your stubborn snake refuses a few scented meals.

Lizards and Snakes

Sometimes a scented rodent still is not enough to convince a reluctant feeder to eat. Often, nothing other than an actual lizard will do. If you only have access to adult-size anoles or swifts, you must improvise to make a meal that will be of a size your hatchling can swallow. This often means humanely killing a lizard and cutting off a leg or a section of its body to offer your snake. This is obviously a gruesome task that many may be reluctant to take on, but it may be the only available alternative to keeping your snake from starving to death. If you do not want to resort to this, avoid keeping and breeding finicky species such as gray-banded kingsnakes.

Some nonfeeding kingsnake hatchlings, especially those of the *Lampropeltis getula* subspecies, can be tempted to feed on other hatchling snakes. Sometimes snake breeders end up with hatchlings with spinal kinks or other deformities, and these can be a free or very cheap option to offer your snake. Track down larger breeders at reptile shows, herp societies, and online, and see if you can locate a source. Often, they will be happy to provide anomalous hatchlings at little to no cost. If you can't locate a deformed hatchling, you might want to resort to collecting a small snake or purchasing an inexpensive snake hatchling from a supplier. Surprisingly, most hatchling L. *getula* can easily swallow a whole hatchling corn snake that is slightly smaller than themselves.

Scarlet kingsnakes (and several other types) often prefer lizards to mice, and it may be difficult to switch them to a diet of rodents.

Once a reluctant feeder is finally eating lizards or snakes, the next step is to transition it to mice. After finally eating its first meal, your snake sometimes may accept a pinky mouse without hesitation. If not, you may need to try scenting a pinky with whatever species of lizard or snake worked the first time.

Hatchling kingsnakes in the *getula* complex, such as blotched kingsnakes, reliably feed on small rodents.

Force-Feeding

If all other attempts at getting a nonfeeding hatchling to eat fail, the very last option is to force-feed. Force-feeding usually is not successful, mainly because of the stress involved in the process. By the time a keeper resorts to force-feeding, the snake may have been starving for weeks while being coaxed to feed using other methods, and its health may have declined substantially. The additional stress of force-feeding on top of all this may be too much for the hatchling.

Have an experienced person show you how to force-feed a snake before you try it on your own. Aside from the stress to the snake, force-feeding can cause severe injury if improperly done. Force-feeding involves restraining the hatchling in one hand and inserting a food item into its mouth with the other hand, using a probe to push the food into the back of the snake's mouth, at which point it will involuntarily swallow. Use a very small piece of food, such as the back half of a newborn red mouse. A larger piece of food, such as the head of a red, may be too much for the weakened snake to swallow, because its muscles used for swallowing will have atrophied significantly.

Force-feed a small food item every two or three days, getting three meals or so in your snake. After that point, offer (without force-feeding) the smallest newborn red you can find. If you are lucky, your hatchling will have regained enough strength to eat on its own. Again, this method is often unsuccessful, so be prepared for the worst. If your snake is clearly not going to eat and its health is declining, it may be best to take your pet to your reptile vet to be euthanized.

Chapter 5

Breeding

After maintaining your snakes successfully for a period of time, you may decide to take the next step and breed your snakes. Before progressing with this plan, you should take a number of things into consideration. Once your snake has laid eggs, you will need extra space and equipment for proper incubation. After the eggs hatch, you will need additional space and equipment to house the hatchlings. You also need to have a source for food for them. Once your hatchlings are feeding, you must find good homes for them. When you have decided that you can provide all the necessary requirements and have a plan formulated, you are ready to determine if your snakes are ready for breeding.

Sexing

First, make sure that you have both a male and a female. There are several ways to determine if your snakes are male and female.

Visual Sexing

Comparing the shape of the tail just past the vent is one way of determining the sex of your snakes. When viewed underneath, the diameter of a male's tail broadens slightly immediately behind the vent and is still nearly the same diameter halfway down the tail between the vent and tail tip. From this point, the tail then begins to taper more noticeably toward the tip. A female, on the other hand, has a tail that is usually shorter and does not broaden behind the vent. The diameter of a female's tail immediately tapers down behind the vent when viewed from the underside.

Visual sexing is not a reliable method and is best used by breeders who have a lot of experience sexing snakes. Some overweight females may have fat deposits in their tail that make them appear more like a male. Also, some males may not fit the typical shape of a male and may look more feminine.

Popping

Another method of sexing snakes is to check for the presence of hemipenes, also called "popping." The hemipenes are the male snake's equivalent of a penis, and they are used for the transmission of sperm to the female during copulation. Snakes have a pair of these structures that are normally kept inverted into the base of the tail behind the vent. This accounts for the shape of the male's tail.

This is a kingsnake being sexed by manual eversion ("popping"). Note the protruding hemipenes, indicating that this is a male.

Popping is a way of manually everting one or both hemipenes out of the vent. This is easiest to do on hatchling snakes, but it is possible to do on adults if you have experience. Because the process of popping hemipenes can cause injury to the snake, you should learn from someone with experience. Obviously, the presence of hemipenes confirms the sex as a male, but the lack of everted hemipenes when popped doesn't always necessarily confirm that the snake is a female if the procedure was performed improperly.

Probing

A third method of sexing, also best left to experienced professionals, is probing. Reptile sexing probes come in a variety of sizes, and matching the proper size with your snake is very important to minimize the chances of injuring your snake. Lubricated probes are inserted into the vent and gently directed toward the tail tip. If the snake is a male, the probe can easily be inserted into one of the inverted hemipenes and will therefore be inserted much deeper than if the snake is a female, which lacks these deep pockets.

Ask an Expert

It cannot be stressed enough that the invasive methods of sexing snakes—popping and probing—are best left to the professionals. Any attempt at sexing using these methods may cause irreversible damage to your snake that can prevent it from breeding. Seek the guidance of a reputable breeder or pet store specializing in reptiles. If a herpetological society exists locally, its members can provide help or at least give references of people who can help you accurately and safely sex your snakes.

Breeding Size

After determining that you have a male and a female, you then must make sure that your snakes are sexually mature. A snake's maturity is based more on its size rather than its age. Snakes grow at different rates depending on the frequency of feeding. It is possible to get a kingsnake or milk snake to breeding size in slightly over a year by "pushing" it with frequent feedings, but many frown on this approach. On average, a snake fed once a week should be up to breeding size within two to three years. Like people, snakes grow at different rates, so it may take longer than this in some cases.

So at what size is a snake mature? Snakes can successfully breed at surprisingly small sizes, and this often happens in the wild. In captivity, it is preferable to be patient and let

Probing is an accurate way to sex snakes, but you must probe carefully to avoid injuring the snake.

your snakes grow to an average adult size before introducing a male and female. This will reduce the possibility of reproductive complications, which seem to happen with greater frequency in smaller individuals, especially among females. Males can be safely bred at a slightly smaller size than females.

The size of a snake is best judged by weight rather than length. Most breeders weigh their snakes in grams. A gram scale is a good investment for a breeder and is useful not only for determining breeding size but also for monitoring weights before, during, and after the breeding season.

In general, females of *Lampropeltis getula* subspecies can be bred at a minimum of 300 grams (10.6 oz), while males can be bred at about 200 grams (7 oz). This includes Florida, California, Mexican black, desert, speckled, Goin's, Brook's, and chain kings. Kingsnakes of the *Lampropeltis mexicana* complex can be bred at a smaller minimum size, with females at 200 grams (7 oz) and males at 100 grams (3.5 oz). Most milk snakes, including Pueblan, Honduran, Sinaloan, and Mexican milks, also can be bred at a minimum of 100 grams (3.5 oz) for males and 200 grams (7 oz) for females.

Note that these minimum weights are for snakes that are of normal healthy body weight. Never consider an underweight snake of any size to be fit for breeding. The stress of breeding and egg laying is very taxing to a snake, and an underweight snake will be in very poor shape after laying her eggs. She also may be susceptible to egg laying complications. A good breeder will have a plump appearance and good muscle tone, but she will not be overweight. If you run your thumb along the snake's ventral surface from its midsection toward the tail, its abdomen should not feel hollow or empty; rather, it should feel solid due to healthy musculature. Obese snakes are often poor breeders, and like emaciated snakes, they may be prone to reproductive complications.

Record Keeping

The successful reptile breeder maintains detailed records of his individual breeder animals and any significant breeding events. He keeps track of every aspect of the breeding, laying, incubation, and hatching processes by various means. Some breeders have data cards for each breeder, and they handwrite data on these cards. Other breeders prefer to use computerized databases. Regardless of what method best works for you, you must be able to devote time to observing your breeder animals almost daily and recording significant information.

Develop a method for record keeping long before the actual breeding season. Start out with information on your snake's history, such as the source of the snake, its hatch date, and the genetics of its parents. The more detailed information you keep, the better. Providing this information to people who purchase your hatchlings will help to show that you are a serious and responsible reptile breeder. Detailed record-keeping systems become even more important with larger breeding colonies. Identification numbers should be assigned to each snake, and accompanying information, such as bloodlines, becomes critical in maintaining genetic diversity.

Brumation

For the best breeding results, your breeders should experience a cooling period. Seasonal changes are often needed for reproductive stimulation in reptiles, and this cooling period will mimic the winter season. With exposure to cooler temperatures, a snake will go into a state of brumation, which is the reptilian equivalent of hibernation. During brumation, the snake's metabolic rate is lowered significantly. It is still alert and doesn't actually "sleep," but it is much less active. Snakes do not feed during brumation, but they still require water to prevent dehydration.

Before brumating your snake, make sure that it is in proper shape. Some weight loss is normal during brumation, so it is critical that a snake be of excellent body weight just prior to this period. A few months before you plan to brumate your snakes, increase the amount of food that they are receiving to bulk them up as necessary. This is especially important for female snakes if they have already laid eggs earlier in the year. (After a snake lays her eggs, her body is often in need of reconditioning, which should start shortly after she lays her

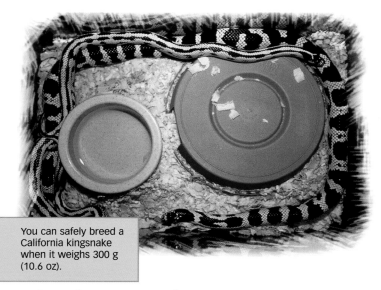

You can safely breed a California kingsnake when it weighs 300 g (10.6 oz).

eggs.) Get your snakes up to a body weight that is slightly more than what is considered average. At the same time, avoid feeding too much, which will lead to obesity.

Two weeks prior to the time you plan to put your breeders in brumation, stop feeding them. This fasting or purging period is critical and will allow your snakes to digest anything left in their stomach and defecate all wastes prior to brumation. Remember that digestion can only take place with warm temperatures, so anything left in a snake's digestive tract will rot when its body temperature is lowered, creating a potentially fatal situation.

Begin data collection prior to brumation. Weigh all breeders prior to cooling, and enter this pre-brumation weight in your records. Keep track of significant dates such as the start date of purging and the first day of brumation as well.

Once the purging process is completed, your snakes are ready to be exposed to cooler temperatures. A clean cage is recommended for brumation, so perform a thorough cleansing after your snake is done defecating for its last time. For most kingsnakes, a temperature range of 50° to 60°F (10° to 15.6°C) works best. Brief dips into the 40s (7° to 9°C) or short periods of slightly warmer temperatures are usually tolerated without ill effects. Some breeders prefer to gradually lower the temperature over a period of several days, but a quicker temperature drop by simply turning on an air conditioner or opening a window and letting cool air in will suffice. Most breeders prefer to brumate at these temperatures for about three months. Some have success brumating for as little as two months. Still others will brumate their snakes for four months without any problems. It is best to not to keep your snakes in brumation for too long, though, because their health will become more and more compromised.

The only practical way to maintain proper brumation temperatures is to turn off all cage heating equipment and cool the entire room where your snakes are housed. Winter is the logical time to brumate your snakes. In some cold climates, simply opening a window and letting the cool winter air in will make the job easy. Close the window during especially cold times and otherwise use a heater when necessary to prevent the room from getting too cold.

In warmer climates that experience fluctuating temperatures throughout the winter, brumation is more challenging. You can open a window at night or during a cold day, and close it as it warms up. If the room is well insulated, the cooler air may be trapped in the room for a long time. Supplemental air conditioning may be necessary if your snake room tends to get too warm during the winter. You can easily provide this with a window-mounted air conditioner unit.

Regardless of how you brumate, many recommend that the snakes be kept in darkened conditions. Even if windows are not present in the room, the snakes will sense the shorter day lengths of the winter season. It is not known if reduced photoperiod or lack thereof is a significant factor in the brumation process, but it seems logical to mimic natural brumation conditions.

Milk snakes from subtropical and tropical areas, such as the Pueblan milk snake, sometimes breed without a brumation period.

Snakes in the Fridge

Some keepers in warm locations have brumated their snakes in refrigerators with success. There are obvious risks to this approach, including dehydration and suffocation. It is best to avoid doing this in a refrigerator used with human food, for health reasons. Use this method only with extreme caution, and monitor all brumating snakes daily, making sure to allow for adequate air exchange during this inspection process. Removing some of the insulation from the edge of the door helps to keep the temperature in the acceptable range and provides more ventilation. The temperature settings on refrigerators should not be relied upon and also should be closely monitored with a thermometer.

Because your breeders will not be defecating during brumation, the only cage servicing required is to provide clean water. The cage must stay dry during cooling. If one of the snakes accidentally dumps its water bowl, immediately replace the wet substrate. Exposing your snake to cold, wet conditions can lead to severe health problems.

Some breeders have success without subjecting their snakes to a brumation period. Brumation seems less critical to snakes naturally found in warmer areas, like Mexico and southern Texas and Florida. That is not to say that these snakes still won't benefit from a brumation period at the temperatures recommended earlier. Seasonal cycling is poorly understood in snakes from areas with minimal temperature changes during the winter.

Even though there are plenty of experiences with snakes successfully breeding and laying good eggs without a winter brumation, there is also plenty of evidence that a well-defined cooling period is beneficial in many ways. Brumated snakes breed much more reliably than ones not put through brumation. A brumation period also seems to help to increase fertility, clutch size, and the possibility that the snake will lay a second or even third clutch in the same season.

After Brumation

After two to three months, the brumating snakes are ready to be warmed up. Heating equipment can be turned back on and normal temperatures resumed. Some breeders will slowly raise the temperatures over a period of several days, while others turn up the heaters and have warm conditions in a matter of hours.

Weigh your breeders, and enter these post-brumation weights in your records. After cage

Male king and milk snakes often bite the female's neck during courtship, as this male Utah milk snake is doing.

temperatures are stabilized in a day or two, you can begin to offer food. The first one or two meals after brumation should be a little smaller than what you would normally feed your snake. Feeding a large food item to a snake that hasn't eaten in months might result in regurgitation.

You will see from comparing the pre-brumating and post-brumating weights that your breeders have lost some weight during the cooling process. Therefore, feed more often than usual to boost the snakes' weight back up to their weight prior to brumation. This is especially critical for females because they will lose an additional amount of weight during egg laying. You want your female to be in top shape so that this weight loss does not impact her health considerably. Occasionally, males will not feed very regularly in the upcoming weeks, focusing their interests mainly on breeding. Therefore, the time before the actual pairing of males and females is the best time to get your breeders up to optimum body weight. Keep records of feeding dates, as well as whether or not each breeder ate its meal.

Pre-Breeding Shed

You will notice that your breeders turn opaque in preparation for a shed a few weeks after the end of brumation. As is typical with some snakes, there may be a reluctance to feed during this time. Continue to offer food in case your snakes are in the mood to eat, but don't worry if they are not interested. This upcoming shed is referred to as either the "post-brumation shed" or the "pre-breeding shed." This shed is an important indicator that your female is ready to breed. She will begin to ovulate and will be most receptive to breeding after this shed. Record the date of the shed. It is not as critical to keep track of a male's pre-breeding shed. Male snakes seem willing to breed any time after they are warmed, regardless of shed cycles, and will even do so while opaque.

During ovulation, the back half of your female snake's body, from midsection to vent, will become swollen. This is most noticeable in snakes of average body weight and may not be noticeable in those that are overweight. This appearance usually lasts no more than a week.

Mating

Assuming that your breeders are up to their optimum body weight (approximately equivalent to their pre-brumation weight), they are ready to be paired up after the female has gone through her pre-breeding shed. One snake can be carefully introduced to the other snake's cage. You will need to monitor the situation closely, because one snake may react with a feeding response and attack its mate. If you don't intervene, one snake may begin killing and swallowing the other snake. A male kingsnake or milk snake will often hold the female's head or neck in its mouth during copulation (often called a "nuchal bite"), so don't automatically jump to the conclusion that one snake is attempting to eat the other. Always keep an eye on the pair for several minutes after they are put together to make sure that they get along.

An interested male may begin the courtship process by chasing the female around the cage, or he may slowly crawl up beside her. He may twitch or move in a jerky manner periodically during this pursuit. Eventually, if the female is receptive, she will allow the male to align his body parallel with hers. Then, she will lift her tail slightly, and the male will curve his tail under hers in an attempt to line up his vent with hers. Once aligned, the male will insert one of his hemipenes into the female's cloaca. They may stay joined together for several minutes to several hours, on average. In rare cases, they may stay joined together for more than a day. Do not bother the pair during copulation. When you notice that they are done copulating, put them into their separate cages. Keep records of the breeding date, and record the ID numbers of the two snakes.

It is unclear at what point after a post-brumation shed that a female's eggs can no longer be successfully fertilized, but breeding should be continued up to about three to four weeks after the post-brumation shed. If you are breeding once a week, you should be able to fit in three to four breedings per female. By the third to fourth week after shedding, the follicles inside the female will have become larger. These may sometimes be easily felt inside the female's abdomen by applying gentle pressure and running your thumb along your female's ventral surface from the midsection toward the tail. You may feel a series of follicles 1 inch (2.5 cm) or so long. It may be more difficult to feel the follicles in some snakes, so don't worry if you don't feel anything.

Five to six weeks after the post-brumation shed (and first breeding), the developing follicles will be close to their maximum size. The back half of a gravid (pregnant with eggs) female may look very plump, and the abdominal skin may appear stretched out. Continue feeding the female regularly to keep her body weight up. She may become disinterested in feeding closer to the time when she is going to be laying, and this is normal.

Egg Laying

Some time between six to eight weeks after the first breeding, the female will begin turning opaque in preparation for her second shed of the breeding season. This shed is often called the "pre-laying shed." When you notice it, record the date. The female will be laying her eggs within one to two weeks after this shed, so it is now time to prepare a suitable nesting site for her to lay her eggs. It is also time to make sure that you have your incubation equipment prepared for the impending eggs.

Create a good nesting site from a lidded plastic container into which your snake can easily fit. Cut an entrance hole slightly larger than the diameter of your snake in the lid of the container. Fill the inside of the container with a loose, damp material for the snake to lay her eggs in. The best option is sphagnum moss, which you can buy in dried bales from many garden centers. This moss can be rehydrated by soaking it in water until it is thoroughly soft. Prior to filling the nest box with the wet sphagnum, squeeze all excess water out of the moss. It is at the proper moisture if you are unable to squeeze any additional water

Here are variable kingsnakes mating. Mating normally lasts for several minutes, but it can take hours.

out of it. If the moss is any wetter, you run the risk of ruining the eggs. This is because the eggshells may not properly harden if they are in contact with a substrate that is too damp. The eggs may absorb too much moisture and will be quickly ruined at that point. Loosely fill about three-quarters of the nest box with moss. It must be loosely packed so that the female can burrow within the moss.

Another option for nest box media that some breeders use is loosely crumpled dampened paper towels. Again, it is critical that you squeeze all the water out of the paper towels. Although paper towels are readily available, they tend to be matted down by the weight of the female and therefore don't provide her with additional security. Eggs may end up laid on top of the flattened paper towels, with only the bottom surface exposed to the moist material. Sphagnum is preferable over paper towels because it doesn't pack down as easily, allowing the female to burrow through it. Eggs will be laid within the moss, allowing them to be in contact with the sphagnum on all sides to prevent moisture loss before you remove them and set them up for incubation.

When you have set up a nest box, add it to your gravid female's cage after she goes through her pre-laying shed. Place the box in a suitable stable location in the cage. If you are providing a temperature gradient in the cage, avoid placing it in a spot that is too hot or too cold. Situate the box in an area located between the hot and cool spot that averages between 78° to 82°F (25.6° to 27.8°C).

Most female kingsnakes lay their eggs within 12 to 14 days after the pre-laying shed. Ideally, add the nest box to the cage as soon after the shed as possible. If a female getting ready to lay doesn't have a suitable nesting spot, she often will lay

Increasing the Odds

Breeding a female more than once increases the chance of successful fertilization. After the first breeding, you should wait several days to one week before breeding your snakes again. This will reduce the possibility of undue stress and will allow the breeders a chance to eat before the next pairing. It can be advantageous to breed a female to more than one male if possible. This way, if one male is infertile or reluctant to breed, another male will ensure successful fertilization. Again, keep track of which males you pair your female with in your records. Of course, it becomes more difficult to keep track of the genetics for selective breeding if you mate more than one male to each female.

her clutch in the only other available wet spot: the water bowl. Eggs laid in the water will be quickly ruined. Some females may decide to lay their eggs on the floor of the cage, where they will quickly dry out if you do not notice them. Without a nest box, some females may simply feel that there is no suitable site and may retain the eggs in her body, often becoming egg bound, a life-threatening condition.

Check the nest box at least once a day after you add it to the cage. The egg-laying process takes a while, from several hours to more than a day. Most kingsnakes will not stay in the nest box after the eggs are laid, so if the female is inside, assume that she is laying and do not disturb her. Check the nest box when she is not inside it. Kingsnakes have been known to eat their eggs if they are not removed soon enough, so be sure to check regularly.

When your female is done laying, carefully remove the nest box. Hold the box level so that the eggs can't roll around. Avoid turning the eggs from the position in which they were laid. Reorienting them in a different position can disrupt further development. The tops of the eggs can be carefully marked with a ballpoint pen so that you can make sure that they are transferred to the incubation box in the correct position.

Often, some or all of the eggs are laid stuck together in a clump. Do not attempt to separate them because the eggshells could tear. Other eggs may be connected at the ends with a thin thread. It is okay to cut these threads so that you can move the eggs safely. Remember to mark the top side of the egg before doing this.

Female kingsnakes must have a suitable nesting box, or they may retain their eggs. This is a Huachuca mountain kingsnake laying

A clutch of eggs that is adhered together also may contain unfertilized eggs, called "slugs," attached to the mass. Try to remove them prior to incubation, if possible. Some slugs will peel off very easily, but do this slowly and carefully to avoid tearing or weakening the shells of any good eggs

Slugs

Infertile eggs, known as "slugs," may be present. Slugs normally look and feel different than fertile eggs. They don't have a white, firm, leathery eggshell, but rather a somewhat yellow coloration with a rubbery feel. They are often asymmetrical and somewhat smaller than fertile eggs. Clutches will be composed entirely of slugs if the follicles were never fertilized. Some snakes lay very elongated eggs that are not slugs, while others appear to be shaped like a typical egg.

Some eggs may have a questionable appearance, looking like something between a fertile egg and a slug. If you are not sure, you should still set up the questionable egg for incubation. If it is infertile, it will go bad and begin to deteriorate, at which point you can remove and discard it.

they may be stuck to. If a slug is firmly adhered or inaccessible within the mass of eggs, leave it there. During incubation, the slug will shrivel up and solidify and may then be easier to remove. If not, it will not hurt any healthy eggs to which it is attached.

Occasionally, slugs will not be shelled well and may rupture during the laying process, resulting in a puddle of thick yellow liquid. If you have good eggs that are in contact with this material, you must clean off the eggs. Wipe as much as you can off with a paper towel, and then hold the egg under lukewarm running water and carefully scrub the remaining slug material off with your fingers. You must thoroughly dry the egg off afterward.

Incubation

Fertile eggs need to be set up for incubation. There are many successful methods for incubating eggs. Some breeders use small Styrofoam incubators sold for use with poultry eggs. Others construct homemade incubators out of a variety of materials. Plans for these can be found on the Internet. Most are variations of the same idea, which is an enclosed, insulated box with a heat source connected to a thermostat. A small fan distributes the warm air to get a consistent temperature throughout the incubator. Because there usually isn't cooling equipment, keep the incubator in a room that is cooler than the desired incubation temperature to avoid overheating the eggs.

High-tech incubators are also available, but they are very expensive. These often have built-in cooling systems as well as heating systems, and also may have humidity controls,

alarms that go off if the equipment malfunctions, etc. These are most practical for large-scale breeders.

Still other breeders simply set up their eggs in an incubation box and place it in a room kept at the proper temperature. If your breeders are kept in a heated room at a constant temperature of 78° to 82°F (25.6° to 27.8°C), it will be easy to simply place the incubation box somewhere in the room for the duration of incubation.

Be sure that the female has finished laying and has left the nesting box before taking the box out of the cage.

Incubation Box

Regardless of whether you use an incubator or simply incubate eggs in a heated room, you must set up the clutch in an incubation box. Choose a container made of plastic and that has a secure lid so that hatchlings cannot escape. Place the eggs inside this container on a layer of slightly moist substrate 1 or 2 inches (2.5-5 cm) deep. Granular, moisture-retentive materials such as vermiculite and perlite are best used as incubation media. These are potting soil additives that can be purchased from garden centers.

Make sure that the ratio of moisture to vermiculite or perlite is not too wet and not too dry. Many breeders prefer a mixture of 1 part water to 2 parts vermiculite or perlite by weight (rather than by volume of either material). Some prefer an even wetter mixture, but it is important to make sure that the substrate is not too wet, or the eggs will quickly go bad. Because eggs absorb water from the incubation substrate, use good-quality water. Reverse osmosis water is preferred if available. Otherwise, avoid using tap water, and stick with distilled water.

To eliminate the guesswork in mixing incubation media, there is at least one product on the market that is pre-mixed with water and sealed in an airtight bag. When ready to use, simply pour the right amount in your incubation box and add your eggs. You can find this product at reptile-oriented pet stores, reptile shows, and Internet pet supply vendors.

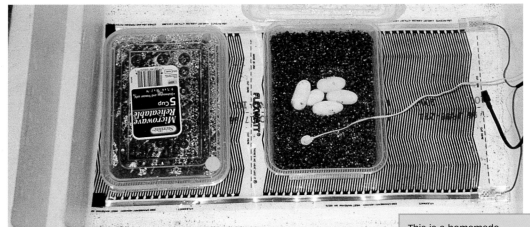

This is a homemade incubator for Ruthven's kingsnake eggs. Heat tape provides warmth, and the eggs are resting in moistened vermiculite.

Gases and moisture are exchanged through the eggshell, so aeration is as important as providing proper humidity. Some breeders drill some small holes in their incubation boxes to allow for air exchange within the box. The disadvantage to this approach is the potential for moisture loss within the box and therefore desiccation of the eggs. The moisture needs to be topped off frequently as needed with a spray bottle. Never spray water directly on the eggs.

Some breeders use an airtight plastic container without air holes. With this method, humidity levels remain nearly constant, yet stagnation of the air within the box becomes an issue. You can alleviate this simply by opening the box two or three times each week and fanning the eggs with the lid a few times to allow for air exchange.

Record the lay date, number of good eggs and slugs, and any other pertinent data in your records. It is also a good idea to affix a piece of paper to the incubation box lid with clutch data such as the parents' ID numbers, lay date, etc. This way, you will be able to look at the data and easily project approximately when the eggs will hatch. With most species of *Lampropeltis*, eggs incubated at a nearly constant 78° to 82°F (25.6° to 27.8°C) will hatch within 50 to 70 days.

Sink individual eggs about halfway into the incubation media. With a clump of eggs, the mass should be set with the lower eggs sunken in halfway, and the top of the clump should be lightly covered with a paper towel misted with one squirt from a spray bottle of water. The paper towel will keep the top of the mass that is not in contact with the substrate hydrated better than if left exposed. Some breeders also use a layer of damp sphagnum moss over the clutch of eggs.

After laying a clutch, the female may look noticeably thinner than she was earlier in the season. She will once again require frequent feedings to get her body weight up to healthy standards. Begin offering food soon after she lays, but keep in mind that she may not feel like eating initially.

Egg Maintenance During Incubation

Throughout the course of egg incubation, check on the eggs a few times per week. If you are using an airtight container to incubate your eggs, open the lid and allow for air exchange a few times per week. If you are using a ventilated container, make sure that they stay moist. This can be done with one squirt from a spray bottle, but do not spray water directly on the eggs. Only use water that has adjusted to room temperature.

You may notice changes in the appearance of the eggs after they have been set up for a while. Some eggs may develop growths of mold on the outer surfaces. On healthy eggs, this will not normally harm the developing embryo inside. Eggs may sometimes be covered in mold of various colors yet still hatch without incident. Healthy eggs that are vulnerable to mold growth are those with poorly calcified shells. If you notice mold developing on these vulnerable clutches, use a little antifungal powder made for controlling athlete's foot to keep it in check.

Some fertile or questionable eggs may die during incubation. These will usually discolor first, may appear to "sweat," and will eventually solidify internally. Discard any eggs that have clearly gone bad. If you are not sure if the egg is dead, leave it in the box and see if it becomes worse or not.

If you are using a slightly damp paper towel to cover the eggs, you will probably need to replace it with a fresh one every week or whenever it appears discolored. Mist the new paper towel with one squirt of water from a spray bottle.

occasionally spoil
g incubation. It is best
nove them to prevent
mination of the
y eggs.

Breeding for a Second Clutch

Within a week or so after laying, the female will become opaque with her third shed of the season. This is called the post-laying shed. This period indicates that the female is ready to be bred again for a second clutch of eggs. Assuming that your snake is reconditioning well after laying her first clutch, she may produce a second clutch. The female can be bred again just like after the post-brumation shed. She will then go through a pre-laying shed like she did before her first clutch was laid, at which point you must add a nest box to the cage.

Despite having poorly calcified spots, these eggs hatched out healthy kingsnakes.

Not all snakes will produce a second clutch. If your snake is healthy, chances are good that she will develop a second round of follicles. If the rigors of laying the first clutch were very taxing on her, she may not ovulate again, negating the possibility of a second clutch. If a female is clearly in rough shape after laying a first clutch, don't force her to breed again that same year.

Most females lose weight after laying their first clutch, but they should quickly regain it within a few weeks of regular feeding every other day. Some snakes that were slightly overweight prior to laying their first clutch will be in very good shape afterward. Weigh your female after she lays her first clutch, and keep track of her weight over the next few weeks. If you see a steady increase in weight within a week of feeding, go ahead and breed her to a male. If you are at all uncertain if she is going to be in good enough shape to go through the stress of laying another clutch, do not risk it.

Second clutches often have a higher rate of infertile slugs, and the overall clutch size may be much smaller than the first.

Some snakes will lay a second clutch regardless of whether you want them to or not. Sometimes, even a snake that you consider too thin and therefore unbreedable for second clutches may still ovulate and develop follicles. In this case, continue feeding the female heavily (offering food three to four times per week) so that she can recover as much weight as possible. If you can tell that your thin snake is ovulating, refrain from introducing her to a male. It is better to have a lower fertility (higher number of infertile slugs) so there will be less effort exerted to lay fertile eggs, which are generally larger and therefore more difficult to pass than slugs.

Even if you never introduce your female to a male after her first clutch, you may be surprised to see fertile eggs. This is because of the female's ability to retain sperm from earlier breedings, which is then utilized by the female when conditions are right. If follicles are fertilized solely by retained sperm, usually at least half of the clutch is composed of slugs, a normal occurrence.

Hatching

If kept at a nearly constant temperature of 78° to 82°F (25.6° to 27.8°C), your eggs should normally hatch from 50 to 70 days after they were laid. In the week prior to hatching, the eggs will "dimple" or fold in slightly, and they may appear to "sweat." This is normal, and it is a sign that you should start preparing your caging for hatchlings.

The first signs of hatching are slices in the eggshells. This is due to the hatchling's egg tooth. Not really a true tooth, it is a sharp, pointed scale at the tip of the nose that is shed shortly after hatching. Its only purpose is to cut through the tough eggshell. After the eggshell is sliced open, there may be some clear fluids and even traces of blood seeping from the slice. The blood is normal and not a cause for alarm. The snake will then push the tip of its nose out of the incision and begin breathing air for the first time. This process is called "pipping."

Your hatchlings may remain sitting with their nose or entire head poking out of the egg for hours. Although you may be excited and want to see what they look like, do not rush the process and try to remove them from the eggs. Keep the box covered, and avoid disturbing them until the hatchlings have emerged completely, which may take hours to more than a day. They need time to

Shell Oddities

Some eggs may be poorly calcified at the tips or have random patches elsewhere that are insufficiently shelled. Uncalcified areas will appear dull yellow and somewhat transparent in contrast to the smooth, white, opaque shelled areas, and may have star- or snowflake-shaped crystallization patterns. Poorly calcified eggs that don't develop mold problems will normally hatch without any problems.

Only double-clutch females that are in perfect health and of a good weight, as this albino speckled kingsnake appears to be.

absorb their remaining yolk supply into their body for them to feed on until their first meal. Not all the eggs will hatch simultaneously. An entire clutch may take several days to a week to completely hatch out.

Occasionally, there may be one or more eggs in a clutch that fail to hatch. If the rest of the clutch has hatched and the remaining eggs are still showing no signs of pipping nearly a week later, they have probably died within the egg. Usually, a full-term death in the egg is due to some physical problem such as a deformity that prevented the hatchling from successfully pipping.

Once your hatchlings are out of the egg, it is time to transfer them to their cage. Hatchling kingsnakes are best housed individually. When removing the hatchlings from the box, carefully scoop up the fragile snake in your hands and gently restrain its body so that it cannot escape. The hatchling's abdomen often will appear very bloated due to the absorbed yolk supply. Therefore, take care not to press too firmly on this part of the body. Some hatchlings will be naturally defensive right out of the egg and may strike or even bite, although this barely results in more than a slight pinch. Pueblan milk snake hatchlings are especially nervous and aggressive, and when handled, they often bite down on their owners' fingers and won't let go.

Hatchling kingsnakes will not be interested in eating for at least a week after they hatch. Their yolk supply provides all the nourishment they need in this time. Make sure that your hatchlings have access to a shallow bowl of clean water at all times. Around a week after hatching, the snakes will go through their first shed. After this time, they will be ready to feed.

Selective Breeding

Many species of kingsnakes are available in colors or patterns that are very different from the typical appearance. Each variation in color and pattern is called a "morph." Many of these are the result of breeding two snakes together that are gene carriers for the trait. Many of these morphs would only rarely be found in the wild, and these snakes often don't live very long because their unique coloration may not help them blend into their surroundings, which makes them more vulnerable to predators.

Although record keeping is highly recommended for responsible snake breeding, it becomes even more important if you take on a breeding project to develop new morphs. You need a way to keep track of your breeders and their offspring to avoid inbreeding and to know the genetics of your snakes.

Genetics is a fairly complex subject, and in some cases, even the experts aren't sure how certain traits are inherited. Most reptilian color and pattern traits are recessive, dominant, or co-dominant. The mixing and matching of these types of traits is fairly predictable, and a basic understanding of how they work is important when starting a breeding project.

Triple Clutching

Some species of kingsnakes will even lay three clutches during one breeding season. No intentional attempt at breeding toward a third clutch is recommended unless the female is in excellent condition after laying two prior clutches. The ability to triple clutch seems to be most likely to occur in certain species, and even then, only certain individuals are predisposed to regularly lay a third clutch. Pueblan milk snakes are probably the most reliable triple-clutching *Lampropeltis* species, but some individual Florida kings, Brook's kings, and Goin's kings occasionally lay third clutches as well.

Recessive Traits

Most kingsnake and milk snake morphs are simple recessive traits and will be the main focus here. With recessive traits, two parents carrying genes for the trait are necessary for the production of offspring displaying the trait. The parents don't have to display the trait to be gene carriers. A normal-appearing animal that is a known gene carrier for a particular morph is referred to as "heterozygous," often shortened to simply "het." Heterozygous snakes are often sold for a much lower price than a snake that displays the desired trait. The latter are called "homozygous."

Several standard recessive traits are known in kingsnakes. One of the most prevalent is albinism, which in reptiles is more accurately referred to as amelanism. With amelanism, the snake lacks the black pigment melanin. Without melanin, the primary remaining

California kingsnake pipping its egg. Occasionally, some blood leaks out of the egg at this stage; this is normal and not cause for alarm.

pigments that the snakes display are reds and yellows. Because most normal-appearing kingsnakes have heavy amounts of black on their bodies, the lack of black pigment results in large patches of clean white to pink coloration in these areas. A tri-colored milk snake with normally black, red, and yellow bands will appear much brighter overall in an amelanistic state. As expected, the bands that would otherwise be black are white, but the red and yellow bands also will appear much more vivid. The bands that would normally be dark red would be bright scarlet to even orange in an amelanistic individual, and the bands that normally would be yellow may be an even brighter yellow. This change in intensity of the red and yellow bands reflects the fact that melanin is present in these areas as well in a normal-appearing snake.

Another trait known in some species of milk snakes and kingsnakes is anerythrism. This is a lack of red pigment and also seems to affect some of the yellow pigment in some cases. A trait similar to anerythrism is axanthism, or the lack of yellow pigment. Because some kingsnakes normally have low amounts of both red and yellow pigment in their skin, it is difficult to determine if a snake is truly anerythristic or axanthic, and often the terms are used interchangeably in herpetoculture.

Several other recessive traits are found in one or more species of kingsnakes. One is hypomelanism, which is a reduction (but not elimination) of the black pigment melanin that results in very vividly colored snakes with extremely clean light background coloration.

Breeding two homozygous snakes together will result in 100 percent homozygous offspring. In other words, if you breed two amelanistic kings together, all the offspring also will be amelanistic. Once you begin working with heterozygous snakes, you will get a mixture of snakes that display either the typical appearance or the desired trait. An amelanistic (homozygous) snake bred to a normal-appearing snake that is known to be heterozygous for amelanism will result in approximately 50 percent amelanistic offspring, and the other half will be normal appearing but het for amelanism.

Breeding two heterozygous snakes together will have more complex results. The offspring of two parents that are both heterozygous for amelanism will be approximately 25 percent amelanistic, 50 percent normal appearing but definitely het for amelanism, and the remaining 25 percent will be normal appearing but not het for amelanism. Because 75 percent of the offspring will be normal appearing and a mixture of definite hets and nonhets, it is impossible to tell which hatchlings are the definite hets and which aren't. Therefore, all normal hatchlings from a het to het breeding must be considered to have a 66 percent chance of being a definite het, because two-thirds of the normal-appearing hatchlings will be definite hets. These often are sold as "possible hets" and are even less expensive than definite hets.

If you have only one homozygous snake and plan to breed it to a normal-appearing snake that is not known (and therefore highly unlikely) to be a gene carrier for the mate's displayed trait, 100 percent of the hatchlings will be normal appearing but het for the desired trait.

Are Two Heads Better Than One?

It is not uncommon to have twin snakes hatching out of one egg, although conjoined (Siamese twins) snakes are much rarer. In some of these cases where twin snakes didn't develop properly within the egg, two-headed snakes result. Usually, the two heads are connected side by side onto one body at the neck, although sometimes each head will have a small length of neck before the split. This condition, known as dicephalism, results in a fascinating anomaly that never fails to get attention.

In many cases, one head is dominant over the other. Some dicephalic snakes do not live very long after hatching because of improper internal development. If they do survive, they occasionally experience feeding problems in which both heads attempt to swallow their prey at the same time. Several dicephalic snakes have successfully reached maturity. This condition is more common than many would expect, although the majority die in the egg because they often have trouble with pipping and exiting the egg. Even though this is not an inheritable trait, two-headed snakes are sometimes sold as novelties for high prices.

The most common recessive mutation in kingsnakes is amelanism, seen here in a Ruthven's kingsnake with a normally colored one for comparison.

Double Recessive Combinations An even more complex breeding project to produce unusual-appearing snakes can be accomplished through the combination of two recessive traits on one snake. Both traits will be visibly expressed simultaneously, often resulting in a very unique appearance.

Suppose you would like to see what the combination of an amelanistic snake (lacking the black pigment melanin) and an anerythristic snake (lacking red and some yellow pigment) would look like. Breeding an anerythristic king to an amelanistic king will result in 100 percent of the hatchlings appearing normal but "double heterozygous" for both traits.

You then want to grow the hatchlings to a mature size and breed them together. The resulting hatchlings will be a complex mixture of genetics. Approximately nine-sixteenths of the hatchlings will be normal appearing, three-sixteenths will be anerythristic, another three-sixteenths will be amelanistic, and the remaining one-sixteenth will display the goal of the project: a combination of amelanism and anerythrism in which the snake lacks both black and red pigments and has a reduction of yellow, often resulting in a subtly patterned white snake that is referred to as "snow."

Among the offspring of this breeding that were normal appearing, some will be het for amelanism, some will be het for anerythrism, and some will not be het for either. Therefore, these normal hatchlings are considered possible hets for amelanism or anerythrism. Of the anerythristic hatchlings from this breeding, some will be het for amelanism, and some won't, and therefore these anerythristics will be possible hets for amelanism. Similarly, some but not all of the amelanistic hatchlings will be possible het for anerythrism.

A few double recessive morphs of some kingsnake and milk snake species are available. Aside from the snow morph mentioned previously, there is also a ghost morph, a combination of hypomelanism and anerythrism. This reduction of black pigment and lack of red pigment results in a very faded snake with light grayish tones.

Other Selective Breeding Projects

Aside from recessive traits, certain unique appearances exist that may be emphasized through breeding similar-appearing individuals, saving the best-looking offspring, and continuing to refine the appearance over time to produce the desired results. This is best done with examples displaying unusual patterning, unusually bright coloration, or other visible characteristics. Certain populations of a wide-ranging species may vary considerably, and anything noticeably different from what is normally available may be a potential selective-breeding project, either to emphasize the appearance or to mix with recessive traits to obtain different-appearing strains of amelanism, hypomelanism, etc.

The many regional variants and diversity of patterning present in the California kingsnake allow for a countless array of possibilities for someone looking to mix and match different appearances. Mix in the many recessive morphs with these combinations, and a breeder will produce an endless number of possibilities.

Anerythrism is a mutation that eliminates the red pigments, seen here in a Honduran milk snake.

Other breeding projects involve breeding two subspecies or even species together. This can easily be done with closely related kingsnakes of the *Lampropeltis getula* complex and can have

Deformed Hatchlings

Occasionally, hatchlings may hatch with deformities. The most common anomalies are spinal kinks. These may be as minor as a kink in the tail beyond the vent, in which case the snake may not be affected, to severe kinks in the body that may be associated with internal defects that will prevent passage of food, defecation, etc. These deformities are often blamed on improper or fluctuating incubation temperatures, poor parental health, or inbreeding, but often some anomalies result from even the most optimum conditions. Ideally, have your vet euthanize those snakes suffering from severe anomalies.

unusual results. Many types of milk snakes also can be easily crossed. Certain recessive traits such as amelanism present in one species of milk snake have been introduced into other milk snake species. These snakes are not purely one or the other species, but breeders hope to eliminate or "breed out" the characteristics of the "donor" over time while retaining the amelanistic gene.

A more extreme project involves breeding a member of the genus *Lampropeltis* to another snake of a completely different genus. Although it is often difficult or impossible to coax distantly related species to breed and produce viable eggs, it has been done. The best success has resulted from breeding with the most closely related genera, which includes the genus *Pantherophis* (formerly or still considered by some to be

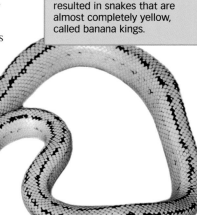

Selective breeding for reduced black pigments in California kingsnakes has resulted in snakes that are almost completely yellow, called banana kings.

Elaphe), which includes the North American rat snakes and the genus *Pituophis*, which includes gopher, pine, and bull snakes. Hybrids involving the corn snake (*Pantherophis gutattus*) are the most prevalent in herpetoculture. Even though most attempts are unsuccessful, some committed breeders have been able to breed various species of *Lampropeltis* to corn snakes, resulting in very unusual appearances somewhere in the middle of the two.

Many breeders frown upon the hybridization of species, preferring to preserve a species' genetics

King & Milk Snakes

rather than dilute it into something that is far removed from nature's intentions and possibly lacking vigor. However, some argue that the breeding and successful hatching of a hybrid can help either reinforce or question presumed evolutionary relationships.

Breeding projects also can focus on selecting for desirable traits that are not visible but nonetheless important to the breeder. It is now well known that certain snakes are predisposed to laying larger clutches of eggs than others. Holding back offspring that hatched out of larger-than-normal clutches and breeding them together later may eventually result in a breeding colony that produces at its greatest potential. Aside from clutch size, egg size (and therefore hatchling size) is another trait that can be selected for. Usually, smaller clutches comprise larger eggs, and larger clutches are more likely to have smaller eggs. Larger hatchlings are often more vigorous and tend to have less initial feeding problems than smaller hatchlings. If you are looking to produce the maximum amount of large, robust hatchlings, select hatchlings from large clutches that comprise large eggs.

A concern to the breeder is the possibility of negative results from a lack of genetic diversity. In the initial development of a breeding project, it is necessary to breed parents to their siblings or to breed siblings together to obtain the initial foundation for the project. From this point forward, it is important to begin mixing new unrelated animals into the project to introduce fresh genes. If successive generations of closely related snakes continue to be bred together over time, severe developmental defects will begin to appear in hatchlings.

Breeders working with Sinaloan milk snakes often select for reduced or interesting patterns.

Chapter 6

Health Care

Kingsnakes are hardy reptiles that are not prone to many health problems. As long as you provide your snake with the proper husbandry, it will rarely suffer from disease and may live for 15 years or more. Most health problems seen in *Lampropeltis* result from inadequate care.

Finding a Reptile Vet

As pet reptiles become increasingly popular, the number of veterinarians with at least basic knowledge of reptile medicine continues to grow. Still, it is difficult to find a veterinarian with proper experience. Many vets still specialize only in traditional pets such as dogs and cats and other popular warm-blooded animals. Don't necessarily go with a vet who claims to have experience treating reptiles, because her experiences may be very limited. The many negative experiences that keepers have had clearly show that there are too many vets who accept reptile patients but really don't know what they are doing. Of course, with diligent searching, you can find knowledgeable vets. Remember that even the experts may not have the answers to everything because herpetological medicine has, until recently, been an area that has not received enough attention.

A good way to find a vet educated in reptile medicine is to search the listings of members on the webpage of the Association of Reptile and Amphibian Veterinarians (ARAV) at www.arav.org. There you can find the closest vet to you who is a member, which means that she is up to date on the latest in proper reptile care. The ARAV is dedicated to improving reptilian veterinary care and husbandry through research and education

Aside from proper husbandry issues, keep your snake away from potentially toxic substances. Cigarette smoke is obviously bad for humans and can be worse for reptiles because of their smaller size. Do not use chemical fumes, such as those produced from aerosol insecticides and household cleaners, in the same room as your snake. After using cleaning chemicals such as bleach to clean cages or cage furnishings, thoroughly rinse all residues off so that your snake does not come in contact with any traces of it.

Reptile Veterinarians

Before problems arise, seek out a veterinarian with reptile experience in your area. Unfortunately, veterinarians with any knowledge of proper reptile husbandry and medicine are few and far between. This has been slowly changing as reptiles have become more popular and accepted as pets in recent years. Pet stores that sell reptiles can often recommend veterinarians, as can fellow hobbyists or herp societies in your area. It is worth traveling the extra distance for good care and advice that may otherwise mean life or death for your pet.

Kingsnakes suffer stress when denied hiding places or kept in other unsuitable conditions.

Quarantine

Always house new acquisitions singly, and keep them away from other reptiles in your possession for at least three months. This is preferably done in a separate room, and supplies should not be shared between quarantine animals and the rest of your collection. Always take care of isolated animals after taking care of any other pets you have, and sanitize your hands afterward.

Quarantine allows for any potentially communicable problems to develop away from the main collection. The health of animals in quarantine should be closely monitored during this time. Some breeders administer prophylactic dosages of antibiotics that target parasitic worms and protozoans. Deparasitization should only be performed under the supervision of a veterinarian experienced with reptile medicine.

Because the majority of kingsnakes available are captive born, the likelihood that parasites will be present is greatly reduced. However, housing these "clean" animals in close proximity to wild-caught or otherwise sick animals (or sharing supplies between sick and healthy animals) greatly increases the risk of pathogen spread.

Stress

As with humans, stress in reptiles can result from any uncomfortable experiences. By

Salmonella

This bacterial infection is more of a problem for reptile keepers than for the animals themselves. It should be assumed that every reptile and supply used for reptiles is a potential source of *Salmonella*. Most reptiles do have *Salmonella* in their systems, but it normally doesn't affect them in any way. *Salmonella* is shed by a reptile through its feces.

Infections in humans (called salmonellosis or simply salmonella) usually cause diarrhea and fever, but can become more severe and even fatal for infants as well as those with a compromised immune system. All responsible reptile keepers must sanitize their hands immediately after handling reptiles and their supplies. Also, never eat or drink when handling reptiles or their supplies. Keep reptiles out of food preparation areas. Pregnant or nursing mothers should avoid contact with reptiles. Children handling reptiles should always be supervised by an adult, as well as taught about how to prevent the contraction of this illness.

meeting all the requirements needed by this species, problems with stress should not be an issue. Although your snake may not show it, you should assume that certain unavoidable events, like handling and egg laying, are stressful to some degree. It is the owner's responsibility to make sure that these uncomfortable times are kept to a minimum and that the snake is kept happy by providing all that it needs for a healthy existence. Negative situations that continue for a long period of time can lead to health problems such as loss of appetite, which will then progress to emaciation and death if you still do not correct the problem.

The proliferation of some internal parasites may be stress induced. A healthy immune system normally keeps the parasite load suppressed to harmless levels, but when the animal is stressed, parasites quickly multiply and overtake the animal, causing death if not treated.

Keep in mind that shipping and transporting snakes is extremely stressful considering how much the carriers throw the packages around, as well as the many temperature and humidity fluctuations experienced along the way. Lack of food, and especially water, for a considerable amount of time also affects snakes negatively. When receiving reptiles that have been shipped to you, set them up in a suitable environment as soon as possible, offer drinking water, and leave them alone for a few days to settle down and adjust to their new surroundings.

Common Problems

Kingsnakes are generally healthy pets when well cared for. They are not overly prone to illnesses, but there are a few issues of which the hobbyist should be aware.

Dermatitis

Snakes kept in a cage with substrate that is too wet and/or too dirty will commonly develop a skin infection on their ventral scales, sometimes called "belly rot" or "blister disease." This can become severe and must be treated as soon as possible. Move the snake to a temporary cage set up with newspaper on the bottom, and change the paper daily. Use topical antibiotic ointment sparingly to help stop the infection. Severe cases may require the aid of your vet.

Other skin rashes may be caused by burns from heat sources. Make sure that you are using the proper types of heating methods, and avoid using unsafe heat sources, such as hot rocks. Also, position any heating lamps outside the cage out of reach of your snake.

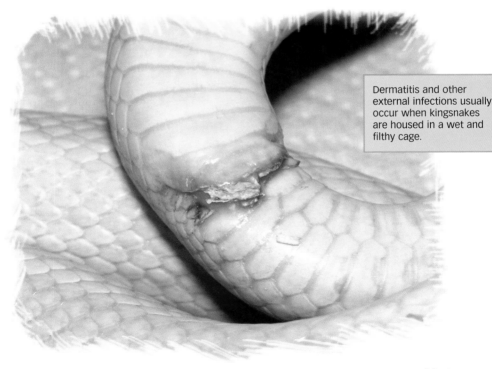

Dermatitis and other external infections usually occur when kingsnakes are housed in a wet and filthy cage.

Egg Binding

An egg-bound female is unable to pass one or more eggs from her body. The causes of egg binding (also known as dystocia) are not really known, but the condition is often attributed to obesity, improper body weight, or a lack of a suitable laying site. Eggs that are not laid when they are supposed to will solidify and harden within the female's abdomen and can easily be felt through the underside of her body, possibly creating a visible bulge.

An egg-bound female with a lodged egg very close to the vent is easier to treat than one with an egg retained toward her midsection. In the former case, the female may be able to pass the egg a few days after the rest of the clutch was laid. Do not attempt to squeeze the egg out of the vent, because this can result in internal damage.

Eggs that have been retained for a week after the rest of the clutch was laid will solidify within the oviduct. Once the eggs harden, the female is less able to pass them on her own. Ideally, seek veterinary care earlier instead of later. Your vet can insert a syringe through your snake's body into the egg and withdraw enough fluid to reduce the size of the egg to allow it to pass more easily. Other methods, including surgical removal, have been performed successfully, but this procedure is costly. In some cases, especially when one egg is retained high up in the body, an egg-bound female can live for quite a while without ill effects; in other cases, the female's health will gradually deteriorate.

This is a kingsnake suffering from egg-binding. This condition usually requires veterinary attention.

Intestinal Impactions

Large indigestible objects or an accumulation of small indigestible objects can become lodged in the intestine, restricting flow of waste and ultimately causing death if not passed. Occasionally, your snake may get a mouthful of substrate when it is eating, which it will then swallow.

Impactions may be clearly noticeable if the ingested object(s) are fairly large, but unfortunately, most impactions are not noticed until a necropsy is performed to determine the cause of death.

To prevent impactions from occurring, avoid using substrate such as gravel or coarse sand that may accidentally become ingested when the snake feeds. You also can try feeding your snake on a plate or piece of cardboard.

Mouth Rot

Mouth rot, or stomatitis, is an infection in the mouth that is usually characterized by masses of caseous or "cheesy" material clearly visible upon opening the mouth. Injuries to the mouth often cause mouth rot and often spread to other areas of the head and become fatal. At the very least, a snake with mouth rot will be reluctant to eat. The best cure for this ailment in the early stages is to raise the cage temperature to around 85°F (29.4°C) and regularly clean all the cheesy matter out of your snake's mouth using probes and cotton swabs. If you are uncomfortable doing this, your vet can assist you. Later stages of mouth rot definitely require veterinary treatment, including antibiotics.

Prolapse of Cloaca

The passing of the rear portion of the intestine out through the vent occurs occasionally in reptiles. There are a number of reasons for this, not all of which are fully understood.

Signs of an Unhealthy Snake

If your kingsnake displays any of the signs in the list below, it may need veterinary attention. If you are in doubt, it is better to seek the opinion of a veterinarian with experience in reptile medicine than to wait and see what happens. The sooner the animal sees the vet, the greater the chance it will recover.

- **abnormal feces—runny, odd color, excessive odor, worms**
- **consistently refusing food and losing weight**
- **foaming or bubbling in mouth or nostrils**
- **inability to right itself when turned upside down**
- **tissue protruding from vent**
- **unexplained weight loss**
- **vomiting**

Egg-bound females trying to pass eggs can sometimes end up prolapsing their cloaca. An intestinal impaction can result in a prolapsed cloaca as well. Abdominal injury also can create this problem, and other times there is no apparent cause. This is an emergency situation, so if prolapse should happen to your snake, consult with your veterinarian right away.

Prolapse of Hemipenis

Occasionally, a male snake will be unable to withdraw one of his two hemipenes back into his body after copulation. Sometimes this can be caused by a piece of substrate or other foreign material getting stuck to the organ, which prevents it from retracting, while other times there is no clear cause.

If caught early, an experienced breeder can sometimes massage the hemipenis back into the body. This is difficult to accomplish and may not be completely successful depending on how long the hemipenis has been prolapsed. Often, the problem is caught after the hemipenis becomes necrotic, and a veterinarian must amputate it. Snakes have been known to successfully breed after a hemipenal amputation using their remaining hemipenis.

Regurgitation

Regurgitation can occur as a result of rough handling (especially soon after feeding), extreme temperature changes after feeding, internal parasites, feeding too large of a meal, or any stressful situation. See your vet if regurgitation becomes a recurring problem.

This is a Pueblan milk snake suffering from an advanced case of mouth rot.

King & Milk Snakes

Shedding Problems

Dysecdysis is the inability to shed some or all of the skin, which leads to other serious problems. With snakes, the retained skin will usually have a dull, wrinkled appearance and feel very dry and rough to the touch. The skin may be flaking off in areas yet difficult to manually remove in large pieces. A snake with retained skin all over its body will be unlikely to eat until the skin has been removed. An affected snake that is left untreated will develop an infection between the layers of skin and will likely die.

Snakes have a layer of skin over the eye that is called the "brille," also known as the eye cap or spectacle. After your snake's shed, you must inspect the shed skin to make sure that the eye caps were properly shed off. Sometimes they are retained but must not be left this way for very long. If neglected, severe eye damage could result, including loss of the eye in extreme cases.

If your snake has a retained eye cap, you often can remove it with the aid of a piece of tape. Gently press the sticky side of the tape against the eye and pull it away, hopefully with the eye cap attached to the tape. Sometimes the retained eye cap will be more difficult to remove. Careful use of tweezers can sometimes aid in removal. If you are at all uncomfortable with this procedure, or if you still are unable to get the eye cap off, it consult your veterinarian.

Sometimes the skin is successfully shed from much of the body but is retained around the tail tip. If not caught in time, the skin may tighten and constrict the tail, restricting blood flow and resulting in loss of the tail tip.

A number of things can cause dysecdysis, but most often it results from dehydration and/or low ambient humidity. External parasite infestations also can cause shedding problems. In addition, skin may be retained at the site of a skin abrasion or bite.

To treat dysecdysis, first assess the condition of your snake. If it is in advanced stages, veterinary aid may be necessary. If it is caught early, the problem can be corrected with no ill effects. Mist the inside of your snake's cage with a spray bottle to elevate the humidity.

Dehydration

Dehydration usually occurs due to mistreatment. As long as you offer your snake water and the proper humidity levels, dehydration will never be an issue. Snakes weakened from sickness or injury may not actively seek out water. If you suspect that your snake is not drinking, gently direct its head into the water bowl. Often, upon contact with the water's surface, the snake will begin drinking.

Make sure that the snake's water bowl is large enough for it to soak in. If this doesn't help, isolate your snake in a secure container with plenty of ventilation holes in the sides, with either damp sphagnum moss or moistened paper towels as a substrate. Several hours in this humid enclosure often loosens the dried skin, which you can then peel off manually.

A kingsnake's eyes become cloudy a few days before it sheds it skin, shown here on a Florida kingsnake.

Superficial Injuries

External injuries such as minor skin lacerations and bites usually heal without any problems as long as the cage is kept clean to prevent conditions that can lead to infection. Monitor injuries closely, and if infections appear or bleeding is excessive, see your veterinarian. Use topical antibiotic cream sparingly on injuries to prevent infections. Apply the cream to the affected area, and then lightly wipe off any excess. Avoid using liberal amounts of antibiotic cream on injuries.

Weight Loss

Snakes often respond to stress or sickness by not eating, which will lead to weight loss if the problem is not corrected. Infrequent feeding and internal parasites also can cause emaciation. Usually, the first sign of severe emaciation is visual protrusion of the backbone. See your vet to determine what may be causing your snake's weight loss.

Parasites

Determining the presence of internal parasites is performed by analyzing a fresh fecal sample under a microscope. This is a job best left to an experienced veterinarian.

Rarely is a fecal sample from any captive reptile perfectly devoid of microorganisms. There are normal populations of bacteria and protozoans that live within the bodies of reptiles, some of which are beneficial and aid in digestion and others that are parasitic but are maintained at harmless levels by the immune system. Inexperienced veterinarians may want to treat a reptile for anything they notice in a fecal sample. However, some antiparasitic drugs are harsh on the body, and improper dosages can cause illness and even death.

An experienced reptile veterinarian will properly identify unhealthy levels of parasitic microorganisms and will be familiar with the best methods of treatment. There are disagreements in the developing field of herpetological medicine, and additional research is necessary to understand and better treat a number of common reptile parasites. A good reptile vet will keep up to date on the research.

Protozoans

These unicellular organisms are among the most commonly encountered internal parasites in reptiles. In most cases, they inhabit the digestive system and are often readily noticeable in fecal samples viewed under a microscope. If present, unhealthy populations of protozoans should be treated with appropriate antiparasitics as recommended by your veterinarian.

Cryptosporidiosis Cryptosporidiosis is a life-threatening condition caused by the protozoan organism *Cryptosporidium* sp. In species that affect reptiles, this parasite lives in the digestive system, and during part of its life cycle, it encases itself in the lining of the stomach. Large infestations can severely inflame the stomach, thickening the lining and resulting in a disruption of digestion, and ultimately lead to death. This inflammation of the stomach usually produces the first noticeable sign of the infestation, showing up as a distinct mid-body swelling. Foul-smelling diarrhea and chronic regurgitation are additional signs of infection.

Many keepers fear that a *Cryptosporidium* outbreak in their collections will wipe out everything. Although it is highly contagious, many animals in a collection where infections are known never seem to develop symptoms. Kingsnakes, for example, seem much less likely to develop symptoms of this disease than corn snakes.

Unfortunately, there is no known cure for *Cryptosporidium* at this time. Usually when

Obesity

Obesity is usually a problem only with nonbreeding, well-fed animals. Close monitoring of your snake's weight and adjustment of feeding frequency will help to prevent obesity. Obesity may be a factor in other health issues, such as dystocia.

It should be easy to recognize an obese snake. Aside from appearing too fat, the skin between the scales will be very apparent, and if the body is even slightly curved, there will be folds or creases in the snake's skin. Some obese snakes develop lumpy fat deposits, especially at the base of the tail on either side of the vent.

symptoms are noticed, there has been extensive tissue damage to the stomach lining. Several prophylactic drugs are being tested to see if cryptosporidiosis can be prevented in reptile collections.

As soon as you note a potentially infected animal, immediately relocate it to another room away from any other reptiles. If your vet confirms that your snake is indeed infected with crypto, the only option at this time is to have it euthanized. Use ammonia to best disinfect supplies and cages that have been in contact with a snake believed to have cryptosporidiosis.

Here is a California kingsnake with a retained eyecap. After a shed, check your kingsnake carefully to make sure that it has none of the old skin remaining.

Worms

Parasitic worms are sometimes found in the digestive tract of various reptiles in captivity. An experienced veterinarian can determine the presence of worms with fecal samples and can treat them with antihelminthics.

External Parasites

Two external parasites sometimes infest pet snakes: mites and ticks. Ticks are normally found only on wild-caught animals, so mites are more of a concern for most kingsnake keepers.

Mites With many species of reptiles, mites become a serious problem. The black snake mite, *Ophionyssus natricis*, is the most dreaded external parasite because infestations spread easily, are difficult to control, and can cause extreme discomfort and even kill reptiles. These bloodsucking mites quickly proliferate and can severely compromise the health of your snake, causing shedding problems, stress, lack of appetite, and death if not treated early.

Quarantine of new acquisitions for at least three months will allow you to notice any mite problems prior to introducing your new pet to the rest of the collection. As soon as you find black snake mites, take action immediately. Relocate the affected snakes to another room far from the rest of the collection. Inspect all snakes in the collection, especially on the head, where the mites often will concentrate around the edges of the eyes and in the nostrils.

Small infestations caught early are somewhat easy to treat, but just because mites have been removed from the snake doesn't mean that there aren't more lurking in the cage and general area around the cage. Even after visible mites are eliminated, eggs will still be hatching out and continuing the problem. Snake mites are fast moving and can travel surprising distances to reach new hosts.

You can use Sevin (carbaryl) dust, a pesticide available at garden centers, to prevent the spread of mites to other locations. Sprinkle a ring of Sevin dust around the cage on uncarpeted floors, and sprinkle a line on the floor in the doorway to prevent mites from leaving the quarantine room.

Although not approved by the manufacturer for use indoors or on animals, Sevin dust has been used countless times on reptiles without any harmful effects. You can sprinkle it on the substrate, and you can even dust your snake with it. The cage and substrate must remain dry for the Sevin to remain active. Avoid getting the dust in your snake's nose and mouth, and avoid placing large mounds in the cage that it may poke its head in and ingest or inhale a large amount. Sevin dust kills mites fairly quickly, but you should treat caging for at least one month to be sure that all newly hatched mites are killed. Avoid reintroducing a snake quarantined for mite treatment to the collection for a few months after successful eradication, just to be sure.

Another effective method of mite control is ivermectin, which can be injected into the snake or used as a topical spray. Ask your vet to determine the correct dose for your snake. Even though this is

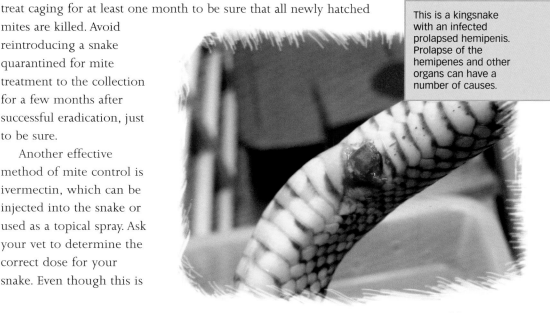

This is a kingsnake with an infected prolapsed hemipenis. Prolapse of the hemipenes and other organs can have a number of causes.

Mites of a Different Color

You may sometimes notice other types of mites on your snake, especially some that are light colored and slow moving in contrast to the faster moving black snake mites. Some types of mites are not bloodsucking and only live on dead skin or dust in the cage, while others may be parasitic. Regardless, these mites should not be allowed to persist; you can remove them by rubbing your snake with a cotton swab dipped in vegetable oil.

very effective at killing mites on and around the snake, you must still treat the surrounding area. Ivermectin is extremely toxic to turtles, so if you keep turtles or tortoises, exercise caution when using this drug.

One treatment that some keepers utilize cautiously is the use of pest strips, which are small, flexible, rectangular blocks impregnated with dichlorovinyl dimethyl phosphate. These strips were originally manufactured to hang in rooms so that the emitted vapors could control a wide variety of insects. In recent years, additional studies have led to the creation of more restrictions on the use of this product for human health reasons. Prior to this, some keepers had experienced harmful results with their reptiles, while others had great success.

Still another method that is not recommended here is the use of pyrethrin sprays. Even though they are effective at controlling mites, harmful results have been reported in reptiles exposed to these chemicals. Due to the current and future uncertainty of these products, and due to the availability of other safer methods, these methods of treatment are not recommended.

Ticks As mentioned earlier, ticks are often less of a problem on kingsnakes than mites. However, they may be present on wild-collected specimens, and they may be contracted from other nearby snakes in the room. Because they are larger than and not as prolific as mites, ticks are easily noticed and removed.

Using forceps, grasp the tick's body as close to the head as you can, and slowly but firmly pull it away from the snake. If done incorrectly, or if you pull too quickly, the head of the tick may break off in the snake's skin and cause an infection. Kill the removed ticks by dropping them in a small container of isopropyl alcohol.

Ticks can also be killed using the same methods described for mite eradication, but tick infestations are not normally so chronic that such methods would be preferable over simple manual removal.

Death and Euthanasia

Should a death occur among your snakes, do your best to determine the cause, especially if you own other animals that could be at risk of a potential disease. Examine a freshly dead snake all over to see if you can find any clues to its demise. Things to look for include skin tears, shedding problems, blood or bloody feces in the cage, etc. Feel the abdomen for hard objects that may indicate egg binding or an impaction. Try to find out if any chemicals were used in the vicinity of your reptiles. Run your hands over the surface of your snake to see if you feel any irregularities, such as broken and projecting ribs, or spinal problems.

A dark blue-green dot on the belly, appearing as if the skin has been stained, usually appears several hours after death. This dot is just the bile leaking out of the gallbladder and absorbing into adjacent tissue, which is one of the earliest indications that decomposition has set in. It is not an indicator of the cause of death.

Here is an obese blotched king. As in humans, obesity negatively affects the health of kingsnakes and shortens their lifespan.

A snake in the process of dying will sometimes open and close its mouth while lying on the floor of the cage, and often it will get a mouthful of substrate in its mouth. Some keepers who find their dead pet with substrate in its mouth may jump to the conclusion that it died due to ingestion of the substrate, but this is rarely the case.

It is obviously upsetting to lose a pet. It is even more upsetting to have to make the decision to euthanize a reptile that has no hope for recovery. A snake with an ailment that your vet has determined is terminal should be humanely euthanized by the veterinarian before it unnecessarily suffers too much.

Chapter 7

Species Accounts

The many types of king and milk snakes are actually subspecies of a few wide-ranging and highly variable species. These species "complexes" will be described in general below with notes on key subspecies, especially those readily available in the pet trade. Taxonomic standings of names are not always agreed upon, and some forms that have been considered subspecies in the past are actually believed to be intergrades. Intergrades occur where subspecies ranges overlap and usually appear to be intermediate between the two subspecies.

Hybrid Versus Intergrade

Hobbyists often use the terms hybrid and intergrade, but they are often used incorrectly. When two different species breed, the offspring are called hybrids. Think of a mule, the offspring of a horse and a donkey. Hybrids rarely occur in the wild, although two closely related species can sometimes be coaxed to breed in captivity. When two different subspecies breed, the young are called intergrades. Intergrades in nature are found where the natural range of subspecies overlap, but the term also can be applied to the artificial combination of two subspecies whose ranges would not overlap in the wild.

Lampropeltis getula Complex

These are often referred to as the common kingsnakes. The northern range limits are from the Mid-Atlantic States roughly westward to northern California and southern Oregon. This range continues southward from southern Florida around the Gulf Coast into Mexico, and west to the Baja peninsula. This species is characterized by its large, robust body that averages around 5 feet (1.5 m) but can reach over 7 feet (2.1 m) in rare instances.

Coloration is usually black with varying degrees of lighter coloration shown as speckling, striping, banding, or blotches. They are strongly ophiophagous (feeding on snakes) but will also eat any other vertebrate, especially rodents. Various subspecies occupy a wide array of habitats, including forests, swamps, open prairies, and deserts. In some places, they are common around areas of human habitation, especially rural areas strewn with debris and agricultural land.

All subspecies are easy to maintain and breed under normal conditions. Hatchlings are robust and usually feed on pinky mice from the beginning without any problems.

Lampropeltis getula californiae, the California Kingsnake

The California kingsnake is one of the most popular of all kingsnakes. It is probably the most highly variable of all the L. *getula* subspecies. Nearly all of the variants are boldly marked with solid patches of black and white (known as the desert phase) or brown and yellow (known as the coastal phase). Intermediates can be found that are black and pale yellow. These color themes are displayed as banding, striping, random blotching, and a wide variety of other random patterning. Some examples of the coastal phase have been bred to be mostly yellow with very little black present, and these are referred to as "banana" California Kings.

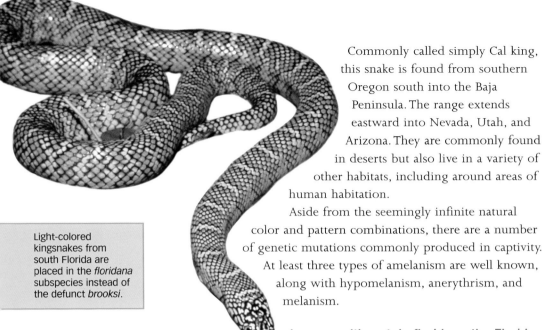

Commonly called simply Cal king, this snake is found from southern Oregon south into the Baja Peninsula. The range extends eastward into Nevada, Utah, and Arizona. They are commonly found in deserts but also live in a variety of other habitats, including around areas of human habitation.

Aside from the seemingly infinite natural color and pattern combinations, there are a number of genetic mutations commonly produced in captivity. At least three types of amelanism are well known, along with hypomelanism, anerythrism, and melanism.

Light-colored kingsnakes from south Florida are placed in the *floridana* subspecies instead of the defunct *brooksi*.

Lampropeltis getula floridana, the Florida Kingsnake

The identity of the "true" Florida king is confusing. Not too long ago, the kingsnakes found in peninsular Florida were known as Florida kings and were considered L. g. *floridana*. At the very southern tip of the Florida peninsula, there exists a much lighter form that inhabits limestone areas bordering the Everglades. These have been known to collectors as Brook's kings or south Florida kings. It was formerly known as L. g. *brooksi*, but later this snake was merely considered a variant of L. g. *floridana* to the north, thus eliminating the subspecific status.

Then, further studies concluded that the Brook's king should actually be considered the true Florida king, *Lampropeltis getula floridana*. The kings found in the peninsula to the north that were formerly named L. g. *floridana* were now considered intergrades between L. g. *getula* in the northern part of the state and the king from south Florida that now earned the title as L. g. *floridana*. This has been difficult for many herpers to accept, and most of the light-colored kings originating from south Florida are still called Brook's kings by most breeders, and the intergrades are still called Florida kings. "Peninsular intergrades" is one more accurate name that is occasionally used for what were formerly called Florida kings and are referred to in scientific literature as L. g. *floridana* X L. g. *getula*.

Three Become One ～ꝋ

Three regional forms of California kingsnake were at one time considered separate subspecies of *L. getula*. The Mid-Baja kingsnake was formerly known as *L. g. conjuncta* but is now known as the "conjuncta phase" of the California king. This variant is dark overall but has very thin light-colored banding. The south Baja kingsnake (formerly *L. g. nitida*) is also considered a form of California king and is dark with a faint light stripe running down the back. The name *L. g. yumensis* was used for snakes found in southern Arizona. These forms may occasionally be available through breeders.

The south Florida king is restricted to areas of limestone bordering the Florida Everglades. Development and agriculture have just about eliminated its preferred habitat, and it is now found primarily along rocky canal banks bordering agricultural land.

This snake is among the lightest colored of the L. *getula* complex. It has an overall speckled appearance because each dark scale has a light-colored dot.

In captivity, a variety of south Florida king (true L. *g. floridana*) morphs are being produced, including hypomelanism, amelanism, and anerythrism or axanthism. Combining these traits, breeders have produced snows (anerythristic X amelanistic) and ghosts (hypomelanistic X anerythristic). Another morph being bred in small numbers has pure white sides to the body and is referred to as "white-sided."

Peninsular intergrades (still usually called Florida kings in the pet trade) are very commonly bred, and there are also forms of amelanism and anerythrism/axanthism. Aberrantly patterned individuals are being produced by some breeders. Many are wild collected from sugar cane fields just south of Lake Okeechobee, although plenty are produced in captivity, eliminating the need to do so.

Lampropeltis getula getula, the Eastern Kingsnake

Known commonly as the eastern king or chain king, this subspecies ranges from southern New Jersey south to the extreme northern portion of Florida. Its range is limited to the west by the Appalachian mountain range. It is generally all black with thin white- or cream-colored markings running down the back, creating a chain-like pattern. Aberrantly patterned individuals with the chain pattern reduced to a very broken pattern are being bred by a few breeders. This subspecies is considered the largest of all, attaining a record length close to 7 feet (2.1 m).

Lampropeltis getula holbrooki, the Speckled Kingsnake

The aptly named speckled king is evenly speckled with yellow- to cream-colored dots on an otherwise black background. Some specimens may have faint patterning of dark cross banding in conjunction with the speckling. This species can be found in a variety of habitats throughout its range. It ranges from southern Iowa and Illinois down to the Gulf Coast from Alabama to eastern Texas.

This snake intergrades with the desert king (*Lampropeltis g. splendida*) on the west side of its range and with the black king (*L. g. nigra*) on the eastern edge of its range. A number of breeders are producing amelanistic speckled kings.

Lampropeltis getula meansi, the Apalachicola Lowlands Kingsnake

This subspecies is new to many because it was only described in 2006. Apalachicola Lowlands kingsnake is the most accepted common name. Some may recognize "Apalachicola" in the common name and instantly think of the variably patterned kingsnake from the Florida panhandle formerly known as *L. g. goini* and often called the Apalachicola King, blotched king, or Goin's king. The subspecific status of this was deemed invalid and was then considered an intergrade of *L. g. getula* and what used to be considered *L. getula floridana*. (See previous entry.) Breeders still use all three of the common names interchangeably today.

Recent studies of the kings from the central Florida panhandle have determined that a localized population living mostly in the

The speckled kingsnake is common both in nature and in the herp hobby.

Hypomelanistic Brook's kings are also called flame kings and are highly prized by hobbyists.

Eastern Apalachicola Lowlands is unique enough to be deserving of subspecific status, and thus was recently given the name L. g. meansi. Snakes from the surrounding areas of the central Florida panhandle are now considered intergrades between L. g. meansi and L. g. getula.

Both the true L. g. meansi and the intergrades are bred by herpers, and both have been called Apalachicola kings, blotched kings, or Goin's kings. Both have been unknowingly bred together over time, so it is best to refer to any captive-bred specimen as intergrades between L. g. meansi and L. g. getula. The snakes from this region (both the intergrades and the species) are highly variable in pattern. All have a varying amount of light markings on dark scales. Some are evenly speckled and are considered "patternless," while others have dark blotches or stripes mixed with the speckling.

Both L. g. meansi and the intergrades from surrounding areas were formerly fairly common, but recently, they have rarely been seen.

Lampropeltis getula nigra, the Black Kingsnake

This subspecies is found west of the Appalachian Mountains, from West Virginia west to southeastern Illinois, and south to northern Alabama. Called the black kingsnake, it is mostly black except for some slight light-colored speckling, especially where the subspecies intergrades with the eastern kingsnake and the speckled kingsnake. It is not often seen in the pet trade, possibly because it is considered one of the less desirable of the L. *getula* complex. L. g. *nigra* might be confused with the Mexican black kings (L. g. *nigrita*), both in appearance and the similar subspecific names. However, these two snakes do not have overlapping ranges.

Lampropeltis getula nigrita, the Mexican Black Kingsnake

Mexican black kings are desert-dwelling kings that are often a solid glossy black color. Juveniles may have faint patterning that fades as they age. Others may retain the patterning into adulthood, especially if they have intergraded with desert kings.

Lampropeltis getula splendida, the Desert Kingsnake

This wide-ranging king is found from southeastern Arizona through much of Texas and south through much of eastern and central Mexico. Most commonly called the desert kingsnake, it may also be called the Texas king. It is highly variable but usually has solid black or brown blotches running down the back, often with a nearly solid dark-colored head. The sides are speckled with yellow to cream color. It intergrades with Mexican black and California kings to the west and speckled kings to the east. Although it is found in deserts and grasslands, it has also adapted to farmlands.

An anerythristic or axanthic morph is being bred in small numbers, and amelanistic and hypomelanistic individuals are known.

Mole and Prairie Kings

This species of kingsnake consists of three subspecies that range from the central to eastern United States. All are

This desert kingsnake has more yellow in its pattern than is typical. The subspecies ranges from Oklahoma to Mexico.

of moderate size, averaging around 3 feet (0.9 m) in length. All have a tan to light brown base color, with reddish to dark brown saddles running down the back. Although fairly unattractive compared with other species of kingsnakes, they do make good pets.

Lampropeltis calligaster calligaster, the Prairie Kingsnake

This subspecies is the westernmost subspecies, ranging from eastern Texas and western Louisiana north to Nebraska and Indiana. As its common name implies, it prefers an open prairie environment, where it remains hidden underground or under debris most of the time.

Although the normal coloration is drab compared with other kingsnakes, there is a highly attractive amelanistic form that is commonly available in the pet trade. Striped forms are also known.

Lampropeltis calligaster rhombomaculata, the Mole Kingsnake

The eastern representative of the species, the mole king is a little more attractive than the prairie king, especially in the juvenile stage when the colors are more pronounced. It is highly variable throughout its range, but the best looking examples have brick red saddles down the back on a light tan background color. This subspecies is rarely seen, spending most of its time buried in loose soil or leaf litter. It ranges from Maryland south to northern Florida and west to Louisiana.

Secretive even for a kingsnake, mole kings are rarely seen except after heavy rains. This is a very red individual.

Lampropeltis calligaster occipitolineata, the South Florida Mole Kingsnake

This is the rarest of the three *L. calligaster* subspecies. It also has the most restricted range, known only from several counties in central Florida, hence the common name south Florida mole king. This population is separated from the range of *L. c. rhombomaculata* to the north, so they do not intergrade, but they may have in the past. Very few specimens are known, and therefore it is one of the most poorly understood kingsnakes. A handful of breeders are beginning to make this subspecies available in limited numbers. They are usually a light tan

Gray-band kingsnake aficionados take great interest in the locality from which their snakes originate. This nicely marked *blairi* phase is from Road 227.

color with darker brown saddles thinly edged in black. This subspecies has a greater amount of smaller dorsal saddles than the other forms, and it can be quite attractive.

The *Lampropeltis mexicana* Complex

This is another taxonomically confusing group of closely related kingsnakes. Although they all share many common features, scientists don't agree that all forms are truly subspecies of L. mexicana and consider some full species. The subspecies and species presented here follow the generally accepted view of this group, yet it is likely to change as more research and DNA work is conducted. Because of this, all species are listed here as belonging to the L. mexicana complex, despite full species status on some.

Lampropeltis alterna, the Gray-Banded Kingsnake

This species, the gray-banded kingsnake, encompasses two forms that were both once considered species: L. alterna and L. blairi. It was later realized that both forms were in fact variations of the same snake, and both types were merged into one species, retaining the name

Lampropeltis mexicana is a confusing snake with a highly variable appearance. Most hobbyists would consider this one a "Mex-Mex" king.

L. *alterna*. Some scientists have listed it as L. *mexicana alterna*, and it clearly has some relation to this poorly understood group. This species is found from southwestern Texas and into northeastern Mexico. It prefers rocky desert terrain, where it stays hidden most of the time.

The snake formerly known as L. *blairi* is today called the Blair's phase. Nice examples have wide orange to rusty red bands bordered with thick black bands on a gray background. This unique appearance makes them among the most desirable of kingsnakes.

The alterna phase has very little to no orange to red coloration as seen in the Blair's phase. It is an overall gray snake with black bands with thin borders of white. Every other black band is broken up into a line of dots, and this alternating pattern is where the name "alterna" comes from.

Both phases of L. *alterna* have the same captive requirements. Although highly popular among collectors, this species is notorious for being difficult to feed as hatchlings and wild-caught individuals. This is because their natural food preference is lizards rather than rodents. They often will have to be trained to eat rodents by scenting them with lizards. Fence lizards and swifts of the genus *Sceloporus* are the preferred wild prey and are the best choice for food scenting if available. It is important to verify that any hatchling gray-band you purchase is eating rodents to eliminate any headaches on your part.

Aside from the two standard phases, the species is highly variable, including some that are nearly patternless and referred to as granite. All phases of this species reach a maximum size of 3 feet (0.9 m).

Lampropeltis mexicana, the Variable Kingsnake

This species comprises many variants that were once considered subspecies of L. mexicana. Many are still referred to by their former subspecific names by breeders as a means of distinguishing the distinctive forms. The most accepted name for all the forms is variable kingsnake, and it certainly lives up to that name. Hobbyists also often refer to them as "Mexicana."

One clutch of variable kingsnakes can produce hatchlings of many different colors and patterns. The genetics behind this trait are not understood at this time.

One of these variants was formerly known as *Lampropeltis mexicana mexicana*. Breeders refer to it as the San Luis Potosi kingsnake or simply "Mex-Mex king." Although variable, it normally has a series of fairly straight-sided saddles running down the back. These are brick red to rusty in coloration and bordered with black. The background coloration is gray with a varying amount of black flecking.

Another variant was known as *Lampropeltis mexicana thayeri*. This form is truly a variable king in that one clutch of eggs may hatch out into a mixture of widely contrasting colors and patterns. This unusual trait is known as "polymorphism." Hatchlings may appear similar to tricolor milk snakes, with black, red, and yellow banding, as well as simple thin black banks on a gray to tan or even orange background. Some may even be solid black (melanistic). Breeding two similar-colored adults together will still produce polymorphic offspring, making it nearly impossible to selectively breed and predict what colors will be produced.

A third variant is the Durango Mountain kingsnake, formerly called *Lampropeltis mexicana greeri*. It is also occasionally called Greer's king. This colorful form has vivid red wrap-around saddles that taper to points near the ventral scales. These are edged in black on a light, clean gray background.

Outer Banks Kings

On the islands off the coast of North Carolina lives a variant of the eastern king once known as *L. g. sticticeps*. Today, this "Outer Banks king" is sometimes considered an intergrade between *L. g. getula* and *L. g. floridana*. Even though the Florida king doesn't range anywhere near the range of the Outer Banks king, it is thought by some to represent evidence of a broader range of the Florida king during prehistoric times.

All variants are relatively small snakes, averaging less than 3 feet (0.9 m) in length. Members of this species have a patchy distribution in northeastern to central Mexico.

Although much easier to get feeding as hatchlings than L. *alterna*, some hatchlings will initially require pinkies scented with lizards. They are relatively docile snakes and rarely bite.

Lampropeltis ruthveni, the Ruthven's Kingsnake

This species also shows relation to the L. *mexicana* complex, although in coloration it is the most distinctive, appearing more like a member of the L. *triangulum* complex. This is due to its tricolor appearance of black, red, and white- to cream-colored bands. It inhabits a small range in central Mexico. It is sometimes called the Queretaro kingsnake. They are poorly known in nature but widely bred in captivity.

Strikingly colored amelanistic individuals are becoming more and more available and therefore less expensive. Like other members of the L. *mexicana* complex, this snake rarely reaches 3 feet (0.9) in length.

The *Lampropeltis triangulum* Complex

The milk snake, L. *triangulum*, is currently considered one species with many subspecies. Because of the number of subspecies and the high variability of this snake, it is difficult to describe. Nearly all milk snakes have banding in tricolor combinations of red, yellow or white, and black from nose to tail tip. Despite these bold colors, they blend in remarkably well with their environment. Aside from the generalized color scheme, the many subspecies and variants in this complex are highly variable. Many subspecies look identical and can only be distinguished by the experts who know their subtleties, such as the difference in the number of scale rows. As a group, milk snakes are extremely popular, with a number of species well established in herpetoculture. There are also a number of lesser known species that are rarely available.

In captivity, nearly all are undemanding and are readily bred with standard methods. Many

Pueblan milk snakes are selectively bred in a black and orange form, called Halloween pueblans.

milks dislike handling and will jerk their bodies back and forth in an attempt to escape, often while defecating on the captor. Adults rarely bite when behaving like this, but hatchlings will not hesitate to bite down on a finger and refuse to let go.

The following are descriptions of the more noteworthy milk snake subspecies and their morphs that are commonly available, as well as a few distinctive subspecies. There are many other subspecies not mentioned for the collector to seek out.

Lampropeltis triangulum andesiana, the Andean Milk Snake

This milk snake from Colombia is restricted to higher elevations of the Andes Mountains up to about 9,000 feet (2.7 km). It is large compared to other milk snake subspecies, reaching at least 5 feet (1.5 m) long. It has alternating bands of white, red, and black, and each scale in the white and red bands is tipped in black. This creates a dark cast when viewed from a distance and a speckled appearance when seen close up. Because it inhabits high altitudes in the wild, this subspecies prefers slightly cooler conditions than are generally recommended for other milk snakes, with temperatures in the mid-70°F range

The Many Milk Snakes

Here is a complete list of the milk snake subspecies, with brief notes on their natural range. Most subspecies are available in the herp hobby, although several are extremely hard to find.

L. t. abnorma, the Guatemalan Milk Snake: Chiapas, Mexico, east through Guatemala and into Honduras.

L. t. amaura, the Louisiana Milk Snake: Louisiana, eastern Texas, and southern Oklahoma and Arkansas.

L. t. andesiana, the Andean Milk Snake: high elevations in Colombia.

L. t. annulata, the Mexican Milk Snake: central Texas south over much of eastern Mexico.

L. t. arcifera, the Jalisco Milk Snake: Mesa Central region of Mexico.

L. t. blanchardi, Blanchard's Milk Snake: Yucatan Peninsula.

L. t. campbelli, the Pueblan Milk Snake: Mexican states of Morelos, Oaxaca, and Puebla.

L. t. celaenops, the New Mexico Snake: disjointed range including parts of western Texas, New Mexico, southern Colorado, and eastern Arizona.

L. t. conanti, Conant's Milk Snake: coastal areas of Guerrero and Oaxaca, Mexico.

L. t. dixoni, Dixon's Milk Snake: small area of east-central Mexico in San Luis Potosi and Queretaro.

L. t. elapsoides, the Scarlet Kingsnake: eastern and southeastern United States, from New Jersey to Florida Keys east to Louisiana.

L. t. gaigeae, the Black Milk Snake: mountains of Costa Rica and Panama.

L. t. gentilis, the Central Plains Milk Snake: central United States, from Nebraska to northern Texas.

L. t. hondurensis, the Honduran Milk Snake: eastern Honduras and Nicaragua.

L. t. micropholis, the Ecuadorian Milk Snake: Canal Zone of Panama into Ecuador, Colombia, and Venezuela.

L. t. multistriata, the Pale Milk Snake: most of Nebraska and South Dakota to Montana and parts of Wyoming.

L. t. nelsoni, Nelson's Milk Snake: west-central Mexico, including parts of Jalisco, Guanajuato, Colima, and Michoacan.

L. t. oligozona, the Pacific Central American Milk Snake: Pacific slope of southern Mexcio south to El Salvador.

L. t. polyzona, the Atlantic Central American Milk Snake: coastal plains of Veracruz into Isthmus of Tehuantepec.

L. t. sinaloae, the Sinaloan Milk Snake: western Mexico, including Sinaloa, Durango, and Nayarit.

L. t. smithi, Smith's Milk Snake: east-central Mexico, from San Luis Potosi south to Veracruz.

L. t. stuarti, Stuart's Milk Snake: Pacific slope of El Salvador south to Costa Rica.

L. t. syspila, the Red Milk Snake: central United States from northern Iowa and southeastern South Dakota south to western Mississippi and northern Alabama.

L. t. taylori, the Utah Milk Snake: Utah into western Colorado and northern Arizona.

L. t. triangulum, the Eastern Milk Snake: Maine to Minnesota, south to northern Georgia and Alabama; southeastern parts of Canada.

(23° to 25°C) preferred. This snake has become more commonly available in recent years and is easily bred.

Lampropeltis triangulum annulata, the Mexican Milk Snake

The Mexican milk has the typical tricolor appearance but has a nearly solid black ventral surface. The red bands are wider than the black and yellow bands. It ranges from southern Texas through a large portion of Mexico. It is a very hardy, commonly available snake. It grows to 30 inches (76.2 cm) in length, with a record of 41 inches (104 cm).

Lampropeltis triangulum campbelli, the Pueblan Milk Snake

Probably the most common subspecies in the trade, breeders and hobbyists produce thousands of Pueblan milk snakes each year. Two forms are commonly available. The typical or normal phase has black, red, and white bands. The second and often more desirable form is the apricot phase, with black, red, and orange bands. The red coloration in the apricot phase may also take on an orange cast. In both forms, all bands are approximately the same width.

Black milk snakes change color as they grow, starting as a tricolored hatchling and turning into a solid black adult.

Hatchlings are much more brilliantly colored than adults. Many adults develop black tipping to the scales, giving them an overall dark appearance. There are exceptions that have a clean and bright adult coloration.

Other selectively bred pattern variations are occasionally available. Sockheads are those with the first white or apricot band around the head and neck region lengthened to some degree. Some breeders have developed strains that are lacking all red coloration. Apricot phase individuals lacking the red coloration are known as Halloween Pueblans due to the remaining two colors, orange and black. Normal phase snakes without red banding, leaving black and white bands, are called Oreos.

This subspecies is easy to care for and rarely bites, but it moves in unpredictable jerky movements when disturbed and is capable of quick bursts of speed, making it difficult for younger keepers to handle.

In nature, it is found in a small area of Mexico at the intersection of the states of Morelos, Oaxaca, and Puebla. It may reach 3 feet (0.9 m) in length.

Lampropeltis triangulum elapsoides, the Scarlet Kingsnake

Ranging from southern New Jersey to the Florida Keys and west to eastern Louisiana and western Kentucky, this brightly colored subspecies occupies most of the same range as the venomous eastern coral snake, *Micrurus fulvius fulvius*, for which it is often mistaken and killed.

Although they appear similar, both have a unique color sequence. Children are often taught the phrase "Red touch yellow, kill a

Honduran milk snakes grow to more than 5 feet (1.5 m) in length, making them the largest of the commonly kept *Lampropeltis*.

fellow; red touch black, venom lack" to distinguish the harmless from the potentially deadly snakes. Some are taught that the coral snake has a black nose, while the scarlet king has a red tip to the nose. This is true in most cases, but this feature may be difficult to see on a moving specimen in the field. It is best to avoid touching any red, yellow, and black snake found in these snakes' ranges unless you are absolutely sure as to the identity.

Curiously, this is the only milk snake with the common name of "kingsnake." It is a secretive snake of forested areas, most often seen after rains or crossing roads at dusk. It is a target species of many field collectors, who often rip apart rotting stumps in search of their quarry. This practice is discouraged because it destroys important habitats for countless organisms. Although actively sought by collectors, it is not commonly bred in captivity. Most specimens available in the pet trade are wild caught, and these are often difficult to get feeding on rodents because they prefer to eat lizards. They rarely grow to more than 20 inches (50.8 cm) in length.

The Coastal Plains Milk Snake

Along the coastal area of the eastern US, there ranges a strange snake often called the coastal plains milk snake. It is found from southern New Jersey and southeastern Pennsylvania to eastern North Carolina, staying well east of the Appalachians. In appearance, it is similar to an eastern milk snake but is brighter in color and has different scale counts. It has red saddles (often edged in black) that reach to the belly scales on a gray to tan background. There is a light collar just behind the head.

In the past, this was regarded as a distinct subspecies, *L. t. temporalis*. Currently, most herpetologists consider it an intergrade of the eastern milk snake and the scarlet kingsnake. One curious fact about this animal is that the scarlet kingsnake and eastern milk snake do not intergrade in other parts of their range, which some believe is evidence that it should still be considered a valid subspecies. Clearly, more research is needed to put the confusion to rest.

Lampropeltis triangulum gaigeae, the Black Milk Snake

This highly unusual milk snake is rarely available in captivity, although a small number of collectors do breed it on a regular basis. Hatchlings are of the typical tricolor appearance, but as they grow larger, the snake gradually turns entirely glossy black. Some individuals

In the vanishing pattern morph of the Honduran milk snake, the black coloration gets fainter as the snake grows.

may retain a slight hint of banding, but even so, they are the most distinctively colored of all the milk snakes. It is also among the largest, reaching lengths of at least 5 feet (1.5 m). It is from high-altitude habitats in Costa Rica to Panama, so captive specimens would most likely benefit from slightly cooler conditions than recommended for other milk snakes.

Lampropeltis triangulum hondurensis, the Honduran Milk Snake

This milk snake from Honduras and Nicaragua is another very popular subspecies. This species also may range into western Costa Rica. It is the largest of the commonly available milk snakes, occasionally growing to more than 5 feet (1.5 m). The red bands are wider than the black and yellow bands.

Other than the typical form, a tangerine variant is widely produced. In this form, the yellow coloration is replaced with a deep glowing orange color, and the red-colored bands are more of a dark orange-red color. This phase is variable, but the overall effect is quite stunning in superior examples.

Aside from these phases, a number of genetic color mutations are being bred in captivity. Among these are amelanism, hypomelanism, and anerythrism. Additional mutations that affect patterns are also being bred, including "vanishing pattern," in which the dark color fades as the snake ages; "pinstripe," in which the black bands are very thin; and "striped," in which the bands are joined into a longitudinal stripe. (The stripe's completeness varies.) Mixing the various morphs together has made a variety of amazingly colored snakes.

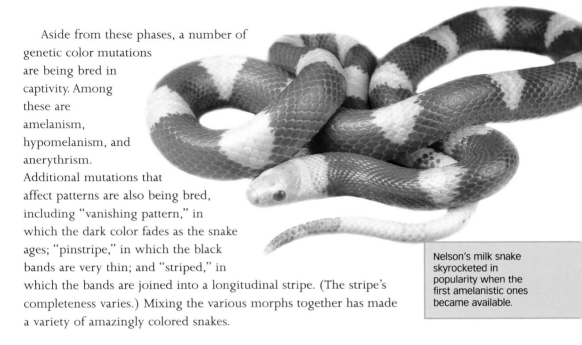

Nelson's milk snake skyrocketed in popularity when the first amelanistic ones became available.

Lampropeltis triangulum nelsoni, the Nelson's Milk Snake

This Mexican subspecies has wide red bands and a thin white band bordered by fairly thick black bands. It ranges from the state of Guanajuato west to the coast and south to Colima and northwestern Michoacan. It may grow up to 42 inches (1 m) long.

Formerly uncommon in captivity, it is becoming much more common, a trend that started with the production of albino individuals. The albino phase is highly desirable, with pure white bands in place of the black contrasting sharply with the deep crimson bands.

Lampropeltis triangulum sinaloae, the Sinaloan Milk Snake

This is another commonly kept and bred milk snake. The red bands are very wide, while the black and white rings are very narrow, creating a distinctive appearance among a wide variety of similar-appearing tricolor milks. This easily kept subspecies originates from Sinaloa, Mexico, as well as some of the surrounding areas. It may reach 4 feet (1.2 m) in length.

A startling patternless form occurs in which the body is solid red except for a black head and a light collar. Another very interesting aberrant morph is being developed in which the three colors are not present in bands but rather in random blotches, some of which are stretched into linear shapes.

Lampropeltis triangulum triangulum, the Eastern Milk Snake

This subspecies is the most northerly ranging *Lampropeltis*, found as far north as southeastern Canada, Maine, and Minnesota, and south throughout much of the northeastern United States to northern Georgia and Alabama. It usually grows to more than 3 feet (0.9 m) long, with rare individuals getting a little longer than 4 feet (1.2 m).

This subspecies is most likely the snake that spawned the widespread myth of milk snakes stealing milk from cows, resulting in the common name of the genus. Although obviously not true, it is surprising how many farmers still believe this and kill the snake, not realizing that it is actually helping them control rodents in their barns.

The eastern milk snake more closely resembles the corn snake (*Pantherophis gutattus gutattus*) than other members of the *L. triangulum* complex. Rather than a tricolor banded appearance, it has brown to maroon dorsal saddles on a grayish background.

Lampropeltis pyromelana, the Sonoran Mountain Kingsnakes

This species comprises five subspecies found in high elevation forests occasionally up to 9,000 feet. The similarly appearing subspecies are distinguished by scale row counts and locality. All are

The wide-ranging eastern milk snake lives in a variety of habitats, from Canada and Wisconsin south to Georgia and Alabama.

banded in white, black, and red. Because they are found in high elevations, cooler temperatures are required, preferably in the low- to mid-70s (22° to 24°C) range in the cooler spot of the cage's temperature gradient. Sonoran mountain kingsnakes grow as long as 30 to 36 inches (76.2 to 91.4 cm).

The Utah Mountain kingsnake (L. p. infralabialis) is the most northerly subspecies, living in the mountains of Utah and northern Arizona. The southernmost subspecies and the one with the most restricted range is the Chihuahua Mountain kingsnake (L. p. knoblochi), found in a small section of Chihuahua, Mexico. The two most commonly kept and bred subspecies are the Arizona Mountain Kingsnake (L. pyromelana pyromelana) and the Huachuca Mountain Kingsnake (L. p. woodini). Some authorities consider only L.p. pyromelana and L.p. knoblochi valid. Other subspecies are treated as variants of L.p. pyromelana.

Lampropeltis zonata, the California Mountain Kingsnakes

This species is broken down into seven subspecies that are found from southwestern Oregon to the northern Baja Peninsula. Most are restricted to high mountain elevations and may not do well in areas of excessive heat. This is one species that needs a definite temperature gradient with a cool portion of the cage for it to feel comfortable. They average about 30 inches (76.2 cm) in length and occasionally reach 40 inches (101.6 cm).

The Todos Santos Island kingsnake, L. z. herrerae, typically lacks any red coloration. It is rare in the herp hobby.

Most subspecies have a tricolored appearance of red, black, and white bands, but some variants lack the red coloration (typical of L. z. herrerae). Without knowing the locality, identification of a L. zonata subspecies is extremely difficult. Even with locality data, some subspecies intergrade in areas, adding to the confusion. Only a few subspecies are regularly kept and bred in captivity, including the Sierra Mountain kingsnake (L. z. multicincta) and the San Diego Mountain kingsnake (L. z. pulchra).

CLUBS & SOCIETIES

Amphibian, Reptile & Insect Association
Liz Price
23 Windmill Rd
Irthlingsborough
Wellingborough NN9 5RJ
England

American Society of Ichthyologists and Herpetologists
Maureen Donnelly, Secretary
Grice Marine Laboratory
Florida International University
Biological Sciences
11200 SW 8th St.
Miami, FL 33199
Telephone: (305) 348-1235
E-mail: asih@fiu.edu
www.asih.org

Society for the Study of Amphibians and Reptiles (SSAR)
Marion Preest, Secretary
The Claremont Colleges
925 N. Mills Ave.
Claremont, CA 91711
Telephone: (909) 607-8014
E-mail: mpreest@jsd.claremont.edu
www.ssarherps.org

VETERINARY RESOURCES

Association of Reptile and Amphibian Veterinarians (ARAV)
P.O. Box 605
Chester Heights, PA 19017
Phone: (610) 358-9530
Fax: (610) 892-4813
E-mail: ARAVETS@aol.com
www.arav.org

RESCUE AND ADOPTION SERVICES

ASPCA
424 East 92nd Street
New York, NY 10128-6801
Phone: (212) 876-7700
E-mail: information@aspca.org
www.aspca.org

Petfinder.com
www.petfinder.org

Reptile Rescue, Canada
http://www.reptilerescue.on.ca

RSPCA (UK)
Wilberforce Way
Southwater
Horsham, West Sussex RH13 9RS
Telephone: 0870 3335 999
www.rspca.org.uk

WEB SITES

California Snakes
www.californiaherps.com/info/findsnakes.html

Center for North American Herpetology
www.naherpetolgy.org/

Herp Digest
www.herpdigest.org

Herp Station
www.petstation.com/herps.html

Kingsnake.com
www.kingsnake.com

Martin Schmidt's Lampropeltis page
www.pitt.edu/~mcs2/herp/Lampropeltis.html

Melissa Kaplan's Herp Care Collection
http://www.anapsid.org/

Pyromelana.com
www.pyromelana.com

Reptile Forums
http://reptileforums.com/forums/

The Reptile Rooms
http://www.reptilerooms.org/

Reptile Forums
http://reptileforums.com/forums/

MAGAZINES

Reptilia
Salvador Mundi 2
Spain-08017 Barcelona
E-mail: Subscripciones-
subscriptions@reptilia.org

Reptile Care
Mulberry Publications, Ltd.
Suite 209 Wellington House
Butt Road, Colchester
Essex, CO3 3DA
United Kingdom

Reptiles
P.O. Box 6050
Mission Viejo, CA 92690
www.animalnetwork.com/reptiles

REFERENCES

Bartlett, R.D., and Markel, R. 2005.
Kingsnakes and Milksnakes: A Complete Pet Owner's Manual.
New York: Barron's Educational Series, Inc.

Krysko, K L. & Judd, W. S. 2006.
Morphological Systematics of Kingsnakes, Lampropeltis getula complex (Serpentes: Colubridae), in the Eastern United States.
Zootaxa 1193: 1–39.

Perlowin, D. 1993.
The General Care and Maintenance of Common Kingsnakes.
Irvine, CA: Advanced Vivarium Systems, Inc.

Index

Photo Credits:

R. D. Bartlett: 20, 21, 26, 65, 83, 105, 107, 108, 109, 110, 112, 117, 120
Adam Black (courtesy of The Gourmet Rodent, Inc.): 50, 60, 73, 76, 80, 81, 91, 92, 94, 98, 99, 101, 113, 115
Suzanne L. Collins: 56
Thomas Crabill: 74
Isabelle Francais: 35, 42, 62, 69, 78, 82, 118

Paul Freed: 16, 57, 84
Erik Loza: 15, 64, 67, 71
W. P. Mara: 23, 52
Sean McKeown: 11, 111
G. & C. Merker: 1, 3, 4, 19, 29, 31, 33, 36, 38, 40, 49, 54, 59, 75, 85, 86, 102, 121, 123
David Scheuber (courtesy of Shutterstock): 6
Karl H. Switak: 9, 12, 44, 47, 48, 89, 96, 122
Maleta M. Walls: 25, 32,